Alethea Jane Wiel

The Romance of the House of Savoy

1003-1519

Alethea Jane Wiel

The Romance of the House of Savoy
1003-1519

ISBN/EAN: 9783744693523

Printed in Europe, USA, Canada, Australia, Japan

Cover: Foto ©Thomas Meinert / pixelio.de

More available books at **www.hansebooks.com**

The Romance of the House of Savoy

1003–1519

By

Alethea Wiel

Author of "The Story of Venice," "Vittoria Colonna,"
"Two Doges of Venice," etc.

Second Volume

With illustrations reproduced chiefly from
contemporary sources

New York and London
G. P. Putnam's Sons
The Knickerbocker Press
1898

CONTENTS

Contents

ILLUSTRATIONS

        * Designed by F. J. D. Lange from contemporary sources.

THE ROMANCE OF
THE HOUSE OF SAVOY

CHAPTER I

AMADEUS VIII., FIRST DUKE OF SAVOY. THE
HERMIT OF RIPAILLE. POPE FELIX V.
THE RETURN TO THE HERMITAGE. (1383-
1451.)

THE strange vicissitudes through which
Amadeus the Peaceful passed, the
positions he successively filled of duke,
hermit, pope, and finally hermit again,
colour his life with a romance totally different from that of his predecessors.

His birth, which took place at Cham-
béry, September 4, 1383, was the signal
for unusual rejoicing throughout Savoy.
His father, Amadeus VII. (the Conte
Rosso), was at that moment warring in
Flanders, where he had gone to assist

King Charles VI. of France against the English, and where he is described as dressed in deep mourning for his father, the Conte Verde, whose death had occurred that same year in Apulia. The French monarch, on receiving the news of the birth of a son to Amadeus, begged him to doff his sables and to array himself in more festive garb. Count Amadeus could find no excuse for refusing; the thought of his own fatherhood must have softened his grief and caused him to rejoice over his son's birth.

This joy, however, was short-lived. The premature death of Amadeus VII., in 1391, left his only son a minor under the tutelage of his grandmother,. Bonne de Bourbon, widow of the Conte Verde. This tutelage was recognised only after a sharp contest between the two widowed Countesses, Bonne de Bourbon and Bonne de Berry, the latter of whom, naturally enough, claimed the right to act as guardian to her son; this post, however, was wrested from her by her mother-in-law, "Madame la Grande," whose nomination

was approved by the King of France and
the chief nobles and prelates of Savoy.
Bonne de Berry, judging it to be futile to
contend longer, retired from Savoy. After
only a few months of widowhood she
sought and found consolation in a second
marriage,—with Bernard, Count of Ar-
magnac, by whom she had several children.

Amadeus remained, therefore, absolutely under his grandmother's guidance
till the year 1398; much of the greatness
of his rule may surely be ascribed to her
training.

In 1413, Amadeus entertained the Emperor Sigismund with splendid hospitality
on his passage into Italy; and in requital,
the Emperor elevated him, in 1416, to the
rank of Duke. It was during the fifteenth
century, which witnessed the elevation of
Savoy from a county to a duchy, that her
princes found their plans of aggrandisement arrested—on the north-west by the
increasing power of the great French monarchy, and on the north-east by the formation of the Swiss confederacy. They,
therefore, with the astute policy character-

istic of their race, determined for the future to aim at the gradual acquisition of Lombardy, which still remained open to them, and which one of their number compared to "an artichoke which the House of Savoy was to have, leaf by leaf."

Under Amadeus VIII., Savoy was one of the most powerful of the Italian states, and could bring eight thousand men-at-arms into the field, at a period when the utmost force of France or England did not amount to more than thirty thousand.

In 1418, Piedmont reverted to its suzerain, Amadeus VIII. of Savoy, in consequence of the failure of the branch of the family which had held it so long ; not, however, before Louis, its last prince, had aided his cousin of Savoy to reduce the Marquis of Saluzzo (who had transferred his allegiance to France), and thus laid the foundation of many subsequent wars with that country. Amadeus preferred peace to war ; but those who wished for his neutrality were required to purchase it. Thus, Filippo Maria, Visconte of Milan, presented him with Vercelli ; and when the

Marquis of Montferrat was hard pressed by the enmity of Milan, Amadeus exacted from him that he should hold his country from him as a fief, as the price of his good offices. In 1416, Savoy was erected into a duchy by the Emperor Sigismund; and Amadeus, anxious to justify the confidence shown him by the people of Piedmont, when they returned under his sway, published, in 1430, his code, entitled *Statuta Sabaudiæ*, in which he embodied all the best laws and regulations of his predecessors, who, even in the midst of their military expeditions, had not neglected the needs of their subjects, but had striven to give their governments something like a peaceful organisation. Nay, Amadeus VI. has the credit of having brought justice within the reach of the lowest ranks of his people, by the institution of the *Avocat des pauvres*, who was bound to conduct the causes of the poor gratis. Amadeus VIII., however, entertained larger views, and seems to have seen that the time was come for the development of a different system from that under which Italy had

groaned for so long a time.   The repeated
grants of the Emperors in favour of the
House of Savoy had done away with the
"immediacy" of the feudal aristocracy,
by which they claimed exemption from
all jurisdiction but that of the Empire.
The counts of Savoy were supreme and
free from all subjection to the Imperial
Chamber ; and no subject could now defy
the laws of the country.   The cities, on
their part, weary of their turbulent freedom, were glad to submit to a more settled government, and one by one came
into the hands of the Prince.   All of them
had charters, which, by the terms of their
ultimate submission, were to be preserved
to them ; but a just and liberal government gave them no reason to recur to
their peculiar rights, which soon grew to
be mere antiquated forms.   The amalga-
mation of the separate townships into one
county, rather than into a number of petty
republics, was further promoted by occasional assemblies of the States-General,
which, though far from being what we now
understand by a representative govern-

ment, did exercise a considerable control, and were probably a fair representation of all who at that time were possessed of sufficient intelligence to have a voice in public affairs. It is a question as to when the "States" of Savoy and Piedmont first began to exercise their special functions. The system of government which Amadeus VIII. established was most thorough for that time. He ordered lawyers to frame and administer the laws; the offices of chancellor, president, and members of councils, and to a certain extent those of bailiff and chatelain, were awarded in consideration of legal attainments. Law lords sat by the side of peers by descent, and the gown became as sure a road to distinction as the sword. He appointed judges to each of the seven Transalpine provinces; and in Piedmont one to every town of note. He held, yearly, a Supreme General Audience or Court of Appeals, for the reversion of judgments issued by local courts, or even by the councils themselves. The effect of all these measures may be judged from the fact that in the time of Amadeus VIII., *justice de Savoie* was a proverbial expression for prompt and fair justice.

Amadeus VIII. greatly ameliorated the condition of his people, and proved his sagacity by the publication of a code of excellent laws. He introduced into his dominions the unity of legislation they needed. He placed this work in the hands of competent jurisconsults, at whose head was his Grand Chancellor, Jean de Beaufort. Thus were produced the Statutes of Savoy, a unique code, divided into five books, officially published at Chambéry, in the great hall of the castle, in 1430. It was from this code that France drew the idea of her own, in the same way that the Florimontane Academy, founded at Annecy in 1607 by St. Francis de Sales and the jurisconsult, Antoine Favre, was elder sister of the French Academy. It is sad to turn from this really enlightened system of government to that part of the code which relates to religion ; there the barbarism and bigotry of the age is apparent ; and the laws of

Amadeus VIII. laid the foundation of the cruel persecution of the Vaudois, which, for a long time, was a disgrace to the House of Savoy.

The history of the House of Savoy is the history of grand military successes and noble achievements ; every mountainside and glen of the picturesque principality has been associated with the gallant deeds and glories of this royal race. Nevertheless, there is a darker side to the picture. The dukes of Savoy, from the first Duke, Amadeus VIII., were always a strong race ; they have produced many successful warriors and astute politicians, and their history has been illustrated by heroic actions and great military enterprises. On the other hand, their history has also been illustrated by disaster, bigotry, and oppression. Kings of France have persuaded Dukes of Savoy to emulate their fanaticism. Though a brave soldier like Duke Emmanuel Philibert has opposed the persecution of the Vaudois, and a conscientious ruler like Duke Victor Amadeus II. has repented of his

harshness, yet Duke Charles Emmanuel
II. has provoked the rebuke of Milton's
sonnet *On the Late Massacre in Piedmont.*

It is strange that the dark horror of religious persecution in Savoy should date from
the otherwise mild and sagacious reign of
Amadeus VIII. But this ruler, with all
his clear-sightedness in temporal affairs,
had entertained a strange ambition to be a
saint also, and finally aspired to the papacy.

The interest evoked by Amadeus VIII.
culminates when, full of honours, he determined to leave his throne and abjure
the world. His reign had been so successful as to be almost monotonous from
the very extent of its prosperity. Amadeus had been appealed to as arbiter by
most of the princes of Europe; by purchase or by negotiation he had acquired
such vast possessions that his duchy,
from a small province, had developed into
an important state; his Court was the
centre of all that was great, learned, and
artistic in that part of Europe; his
schemes for his country's aggrandisement
had always succeeded; yet Amadeus

VIII., the Solomon, as he was called, of his age, determined to withdraw from the position created by his talents and filled by him to perfection, in order to seek the retirement of the hermitage of Ripaille.

The strangeness of the step raised a string of surmises as to the motive of the Duke's act. While one hypothesis pleaded religion as the cause, another was immediately put forth urging worldly grounds. One of the chief motives brought forward was Amadeus's grief for the loss of his wife, Mary of Burgundy. To this was also added his disgust with human nature, as manifested in an attempt on his life by one of his own subjects, on whom he had conferred many favours.[1] A cause mentioned by Monod (one of Amadeus's chief panegyrists), was the influence exercised on the Duke by his niece, Margaret of Savoy, widow of Theodore, Marquis of Montferrat. After her husband's death, this Princess retired from the world among the Sisters of St. Dominic, at Alba ; she refused all the allurements of the

[1] P. Monod, *Amadeus Pacificus*, p. 18. Taurini, 1624.

Duke of Milan, who, seconded by the Pope, tried by every means in his power to make her his wife.   Such piety was supposed to have had an effect in stimulating Amadeus to adopt a similar course of renunciation.

On the other hand, Amadeus's detractors ascribe other motives to his act of semi-abdication.   They refuse to recognise any religious intention in the step, and maintain that it was solely the result of strategy.   They declare that the Duke, in view of the schisms then raging in the Church, foresaw the possibilities that might some day place the triple crown upon his head, and that with this before him he judged it advisable to assume a character of holiness, certain that an outward form of godliness, joined to his rank and his reputation for wisdom, would gain for him the desired end.   They dwell on the ambition that was the ruling passion of Amadeus's actions, and lay the charge of that quality at his door as though it were a crime.   Not quite justly, perhaps, for though an idea of personal advantage may have entered into Amadeus's motives, there is no doubt that the strong element of religion which coloured the age in which he lived reacted upon his own actions as well. The son of the Conte Rosso, and the grandson of the Conte Verde, Amadeus must have inherited some of his forefathers' spirit of chivalry; the matter-of-fact prosperity of his reign may have urged him to vary his latter years with incidents far more startling in their originality than an expedition to Constantinople, or a crusade against the Infidel. The picture of a Duke of Savoy stepping aside from the course of his natural career to retire awhile from the world, only to reappear as Pope, is as quaint and unexpected as can be found in history or fiction; and posterity must marvel concerning the impulses at work within a man who had always seemed a model of common sense, practical rather than romantic, prosaic rather than visionary. Was it ambition? Was it religion? Or was it rather a blending of both of these elements in a mind from early youth imbued with religious tendencies and steeped in that devotion and esteem for holy things which in those days formed a marked feature in men's lives?

On the 7th of November, 1434, the ceremony took place whereby Amadeus VIII. renounced his duchy and retired to a life of simplicity and seclusion. He assembled the chief prelates and barons of his

SEAL OF DUKE AMADEUS VIII.

duchy, and seated on a throne, his sons Louis and Philip standing on either side of him, Humbert the Bastard of Savoy and two ducal marshals at his feet, he related, in a lengthy peroration, all that he had done for the State since he came into

power. He then announced his intention
of retiring from the world, naming as his
lieutenant-general in his stead his eldest
son, Louis, who, kneeling before his father, received from him his parental blessing, together with the instructions as to
his powers of office. The restrictions as
to what he might *not* do far exceeded
the prerogatives vouchsafed to him. He
might form no alliances, engage in no
wars, name no bishops, confer no titles
without the express consent of his father;
the homage, the oaths, and the other acts
of fealty were to be accepted and received
in Amadeus's name only. The Prince, in
fact, was to have all the burden of reigning without any of its compensations; and
the constant repetition of "We also ex-
pressly forbid," or, "You shall not pre-
sume to do," rings with a tone of authority which completely fettered all liberty
of action on the lieutenant-general's part.
Amadeus then instituted Louis a Knight
of the Order of the Collar and bestowed
on him the title of Prince of Piedmont—a
title since then always borne by the eldest

sons of the dukes of Savoy. This ceremony ended, the assembly was dismissed,
and Amadeus remained alone with the six
companions whom he had chosen to share
his hermitage with him. These companions were men advanced in years, who
had been either ambassadors, generals, or
privy councillors ; they were either widow-
ers or celibates, and had already agreed to
participate in the life of seclusion to which
Amadeus had invited them.

The following day, in the Church of
Ripaille (founded and endowed by Am-
deus VIII. and dedicated by him to the
order of St. Augustine), the Prior of the
monastery arrayed the Duke and his six
comrades in the dress of hermits ; and
thus arose the order known at first as that
of "the Knights Hermit of St. Maurice."
Its original character was half religious
and half military, while the knights formed,
in reality, Amadeus's council of state, as
he not only directed from his retreat all the
administration of home affairs, but busied
himself with the politics of the rest of
Europe as well.

The following description given by Æneas Silvius Piccolomini[1] will best serve to show the life led by Amadeus and his knights, the site chosen by them for their retreat, the dress they wore, their food and occupations :

"Far from the clang of arms, with his kingdom centred in the mountains, Amadeus was called upon to arbitrate, now for this one, now for the other, and was considered the only one capable of dictating uprightly, whether for himself or for others ; while to him, as to another Solomon, French and Italians alike appealed. On the shores of Lake Leman many a high and stately tree reared itself above the meadows which stretched away below these woods, watered here and there with running brooks. Much of this land was enclosed by walls built by Amadeus VIII., and within were collected stags, does, and other animals that war not against mankind. Near to the shore of the lake he had built a church, wherein he placed priests,

---

[1] In his *Commentarii*, lib. vii., which were published under the name of " Jean Gobelin," his amanuensis.

and instituted prebends and other dignitaries, and also built habitations where the
Canons could dwell in comfort ; and not
far from there he built a fine palace, having towers and a moat, in which there
were seven habitations, six being similar
and fit to be occupied by cardinals ; in
each one there were a hall, a room, an an-
teroom, and certain secret rooms or re-
ceptacles where precious things were
stored.   The   seventh   habitation,   set
apart for the Prince, would not have been
deemed unfit for a king, or for the Supreme Pontiff.   Here dwelt Amadeus
and his six councillors (*ottimati*), advanced in years, of the same age ; each
had reached the age of sixty.   As they
had all been cavalry officers and had
often led their followers to war, they
now, under Amadeus, Deacon and Master, by the alteration of their secular garb
made profession of becoming Knights
of St. Maurice.   Not far from that spot,
St. Maurice, with the Theban legion,
had suffered martyrdom for the name of
Christ.

" The spot was called Ripaille, and was distant from Thonon about a thousand paces. The Cardinal of Santa Croce, while on his way to France to treat for peace a second time, arrived here with his ships. Amadeus went to meet him at the port, walking down through the woods, girt with walls, to the port near the shore. It was a wonderful thing, which posterity will hardly credit, to see the reception of the Apostolic Legate by this Prince, the most mighty of his age, feared alike by French and Italians, who was wont to be decked in golden robes and surrounded by others clad in purple, preceded by bearers with axes and followed by hosts of armed and powerful retainers, now preceded only by six hermits and a few priests in vile raiment. A company worthy to be admired! Each hermit had on his breast a gold cross, the only sign he still retained of nobility ; in all else he showed his disdain of the world. The Cardinal and Amadeus embraced each other with much charity ; nor could the Cardinal sufficiently extol the conversion of the Prince."

The life of Amadeus there was simple, though not austere. His hours were passed between the wise discussion of public affairs and the close observance of religious exercises with his six seigniors who formed with him the new order of religious chivalry.   Each companion of the Order wore a long beard, as was the wont with hermits, a grey habit with a golden girdle, a furred mantle decorated with a gold cross, a crimson bonnet, and a long, pointed grey hood, and carried in his hand a knotted and twisted stick.

According to M. Jules Vuy the correspondence of Amadeus VIII. with the Duke Louis, his son, at the moment of the affair of Milan, showed unmistakably that the solitude of Ripaille was not one of futile indolence and vulgar leisure, but, on the contrary, full of serious and high preoccupations.

The contemporaries of Amadeus, with two exceptions, bear testimony to the respectable and useful lives of himself and his knights. The attacks, however, of these two pamphleteers, who were in the pay of his enemies, were preserved by Duclos in his *History of Louis XI.* and by Richelet, and were popularised by the malicious verses of Voltaire.

The fare of these recluses was not of a nature to raise uneasiness as to its sufficiency or quality, for one account asserts that they lived on partridges, pheasants, and capons, while pomegranates, oranges, and other fruits supplied the dessert for the hermitage. Many accusations are rife that this profession of self-denial was an excuse for a life of ease, pleasure, and sensuality. It has been asserted that the expression *faire Ripaille* (*i. e.,* to feast, or live well), was derived from the time and doings of Amadeus VIII. and his boon companions.

The opportunity to have a fling at royalty and religion afforded by the charges laid at Amadeus's door was one not to be neglected by Voltaire, and the following lines show his sentiments with regard to the Duke of Savoy at Ripaille :

" Ripaille, je te vois ; Ô bizarre Amédée,
    Est-il vrai que dans ces beax lieux,

Des soins et des grandeurs écartant toute idée,
Tu vécus en vrai sage, en vrai voluptueux,
Et, que, lassé bientôt de ton doux hermitage,
Tu voulus être pape et cessas d'être sage ?" [1]

These charges, brought in later days against a man who in his lifetime stood so high in public estimation, are not worthy of credence. When one considers the extraordinary deference paid to the Hermit-Duke by the other princes of Europe, and the respect which he inspired in men capable of passing an impartial judgment, together with the known veneration and love he had shown from his earliest days for religion, they tend to give the lie to many of the accusations brought against him. His existence at Ripaille was far from being idle or self-centred, though unfettered by the outward cares and paraphernalia of State ; he attended, as before his renunciation, to the administration of his duchy and, in all but external appearance, acted as the ruler of Savoy.

For five years this life of peace and privacy, of activity and usefulness, went on

[1] Voltaire, Epitre 75.

uninterruptedly, but at the end of that time a startling change came to disturb Amadeus the Peaceful.

To explain the causes of this change, we must turn, for a moment, from the affairs of Savoy to the disturbances in the Church. In order, however, to have a just appreciation of the historical movement of the time, which gave the opportunity to Amadeus VIII. of Savoy to step out from a life in which he was quietly vegetating at his hermitage of Ripaille to the most important and conspicuous station in the centre of the stage of current history, we must regard the situation, not only in its ecclesiastical bearings, but also as a crisis in European politics.

The councils which had been convened by different popes to regulate the disorders in the Church had sat successively at Constance, Pavia, Siena, and lastly at Basle, where the reigning Pope, Eugenius IV., had confirmed the Council appointed by his predecessor, Martin V. The Council of Basle was not so much busied with theological and doctrinal controversy as with politics pure and simple. The drama of events had so disposed the principal contestants that against Italy, or rather against the Italian domination of the Church and the consequent influence of Italy upon European affairs, were ranged the other Powers of Europe. The Emperor of Germany and the King of France, with some other rulers, vigorously opposed the Italian policy which ruled the Church and so overruled the nations.

Pope Eugenius claimed that it was the duty of a pope to preserve the Church patrimony even by war, rather than that, without an armed resistance, he should suffer the temporalities of the Church to be alienated. The military conflicts in which he engaged with various Italian princes drove him out of Rome for a time. He passed most of his period of exile at Florence.

Though the Council of Basle had been opened in July, 1431, no sittings had been held till the following December, when certain measures for the reform of abuses

met with only the partial approbation of
Eugenius IV., who also began to cavil at
the nominations of some of the cardinals
made by his predecessor. Thus were
sown the seeds of irritation and misunder-
standing between himself and the Council
that, shortly after, bore such bitter fruit.
The Pope was distracted with care, war,
and the Council of Basle. This assembly, begun by decree of Pope Martin, in-
creased daily by the conflux of the princes
of Spain, France, Germany, and Hungary.
These princes referred the care of all Christendom to the Council; this became intolerable, so the Pope contrived means
to dissolve it. But the Emperor of Germany upheld the princes and prelates
then at Basle. Thus the Council not
only disobeyed the Pope, but admonished
him several times to come himself, with
his cardinals, to Basle, which was a con-
venient place that Pope Martin had chosen
to hold the Council in. Otherwise, they
threatened to oppose him as a prevaricat-
ing and obstinate person.

In order to obtain a greater hold upon

the assembly, the Pope meditated remov-
ing the Council to Ferrara, where he could
very easily force an acquiescence in his
views that was not feasible at the distant
town of Basle. The mere mention of such a
removal ruffled the temper of the Fathers
of the Church, who promulgated a decree,
which had emanated originally from Constance, to the effect that the Pope must be
subservient to the Council. To this an-
nouncement Eugenius answered by annul-
ling the Council, depriving the Cardinal
Giuliano of the Legation conferred on him
by Martin V., and ordering the cardinals
and bishops assembled at Basle to present
themselves within the next eighteen
months at Ferrara.

All the chief princes of Europe protested against this arbitrary action on the
part of the Pope; finally, overcome by
the resistance of so many potentates, and
convinced by two letters from Cardinal
Giuliano (which breathe a spirit of Apostolic freedom), the Pope was induced to
reconfirm the Council of Basle by a new
bull. But the Fathers, quietly ignor-

ing this *amende honorable* of the Pontiff,
proceeded to ventilate their grievances
against His Holiness, and dwelt more fully
than before upon his inability to annul the
assembly, or to convene one in another
place.   Enraged beyond measure at this
behaviour, Eugenius again changed his
mind; he revoked his conciliatory bull, and
annulled the Council a second time, sum-
moning it to meet anew at Ferrara. Thereupon the Fathers determined to act on
their own account, and published an edict ;
they declared themselves rightfully convoked, assisted by the Holy Spirit, endued
with the lawful authority of a regularly
convened assembly; on the strength of
these powers they implored Eugenius to
reconsider his verdict, warning him that
should he not hearken to their admonitions
they would be obliged to provide for the
wants of the Church, and proceed in due
form to depose him.   Their next step was
to insure the independence and superiority
of the Council, and to announce that, if
within a given time the Pope did not
acknowledge the Council, he should be de-

clared contumacious and no heed would be taken of his opposition. These decrees they took pains to establish by orthodox means.

All this time the Pope's wars were continuing. Having recovered Rome, he sent his General, Viteleschus, who sacked many towns formerly belonging to the Church, and sent such inhabitants as survived to Rome. In 1435, Eugenius left Florence and resided at Bologna, where he built a fort and fortified the city.

Philip, Duke of Milan, was displeased because the Florentines, by the help and persuasion of Pope Eugenius, had sent Francis Sforza to aid the Venetians. Out of revenge he induced the leaders of the Council of Basle to cite Eugenius before them. They did so repeatedly. The Pope, somewhat taken aback at these proceedings, made different overtures to the Fathers, to which, however, they refused to hearken. Then, in order to heal the division between himself and the Council, he applied to Amadeus of Savoy, whose peaceable disposition and rectitude of pur-

NICÆA CIVITAS

VIEW OF NICE IN 1726.

pose he had already experienced on former occasions, before matters became so serious.   Eugenius had confidence in the Duke of Savoy, although he knew that he was the strongest representative whom the clerical politicians of Basle could put forth as the champion of their rights.

On account of the peculiar location of the site of the Council, the subjects of Amadeus constituted a majority of its members. Amadeus was one of the most powerful rulers of Europe.   The alliances of his House bound to his interests, by the ties of consanguinity, all the great Powers. No other man of prominence in both ecclesiastical and state affairs was able by reason of the prestige of his position and the influence of his connexions to stand forth as the mediator between Pope Eugenius and the Council.   When it was suggested by the Savoyards in the Council that the services of Amadeus could be utilised, the hint was received with enthusiastic acclaim. At the request of the Council there was sent to the Pope a legation from Amadeus. This was a proceeding which involved

complications of the most delicate character. It was a difficult thing to be able,
in the Pope's presence, to gracefully excuse the action of the Council; for it was

COAT OF ARMS OF HOUSE OF SAVOY, WITH THE QUARTERINGS
OF SAXONY, SAVOY, CHABLAIS AND AOSTA, PIEDMONT,
JERUSALEM, CYPRUS, ARMENIA, LUSIGNAN, AOSTA,
SUSA, BAUGÉ, VAUD, NICE, AND FAUCIGNY.

this Council that had deposed him. They
proffered the services of Amadeus as mediator between Eugenius and the recal-
citrant prelates and clerics at Basle.

Amadeus willingly set himself to the
task ; he started at once for Dijon to entreat the Duke of Burgundy, who was
there at that moment, to join with him in
pacifying the Fathers in Council. Not
content with that, he despatched the
Bishop of Belley and the Prior of St.
Dominic at Chambéry as ambassadors to
Basle, to induce all to lay aside their con-
tentions and to combine for the good of
Christianity in preaching peace and good-
will to men.

It is curious to note how, in the midst
of his zeal for the cause of Church unity,
Amadeus was not forgetful of his own
rank and dignity, and enjoined on his ambassadors, or orators as they were called,
the need of bespeaking a suitable seat for
themselves in the Council Chamber. He
impressed on them what an easy matter
this would be before the arrival of the
Duke of Burgundy's ambassadors ; for, if
the Burgundians were once on the spot, it
would be impossible to precede them ; but,
at the same time, it would be absolutely
indecorous for Savoy to give place to Bur-

gundy.   Amadeus had only lately been
raised to the dignity of Duke of Savoy,
but he argued that, as his ancestors had
for three centuries borne the title of Duke
of Aosta and of the Chablais, the patent
of Duke was not of recent creation, and
his rank therefore should be recognised as
above that of the Duke of Burgundy.   But
this was asking just a little too much;
and thereupon arose the discussion as
to the appropriate seat for the orators
of Savoy.   The President of the Council, the Archbishop of Ostia, occupied of
course the seat of honour; the next highest place was immediately on his right
hand, and this had been destined for the
Burgundian orators.   On the President's
left sat the Patriarch of Alexandria, and
on the Patriarch's left was the seat appointed for the ambassadors of Amadeus.
The burning question was now mooted as
to whether this place was, indeed, the
most honourable after that occupied by
the Burgundians, or whether a seat to their
right would not have been of a higher
grade.   The agitation over this matter

was great, and it could only be settled by taking the votes of the assembly. The relief experienced all round must have been untold when, without one dissenting voice, the left hand of the Alexandrian Patriarch was proclaimed to rank directly after the right hand of the President; so that no slight was put upon the Savoyard orators, and the small superiority accorded to those of Burgundy could not offend mortally the dignity of their neighbours of Savoy.

The importance assigned to so petty a matter causes one to wonder how momentous affairs could ever have obtained sufficient hearing; but there was involved a deeper issue in the question than at first sight appears, which places it in a light not at all comic or contemptible. Amadeus was anxious to rank Savoy among the foremost powers of Europe. He had advanced his country to a height never previously attained, and he was eager to insure for it a position that should be recognised throughout Christendom. So his directions may be credited to a serious purpose, inspired by zeal for his country's advancement, and the determination to neglect no means whereby her position should be rightly understood and respected.

But, apart from the schemes for his country's progress and his desire to promote her weal, Amadeus was sincerely engrossed in the vexed question of the Pope's discord with the Basilean Fathers. His intervention, however, failed to do more than to produce a momentary lull in the strife ; neither the number of councils convened, nor the experiment of changing their places of meeting, proved of the least service in allaying the growing discord. The irritation was too real and widespread ; the spirits of all concerned were too antagonistic to listen to appeals for forbearance and submission. Eugenius declared the Council of Basle to be void : the members of the Council, in their turn, denounced the Pope as contumacious and incapable of all jurisdiction, whether temporal or spiritual ; they passed a decree (June 25, 1439) whereby Eugenius IV.

was deposed from the papal chair, and pronounced a disturber of the peace and of ecclesiastical unity, simoniacal, perjured, incorrigible, a schismatic, and a heretic.

The most learned and able theologians of Europe were to be found in the Council of Basle. The important position of this assembly may be seen from the fact that the ambassadors of the Emperor of Germany, and of the King of France, the Bishop of Lubeck, and the Archbishop of Tours, approved the act of the Council in suspending Pope Eugenius IV., and declaring him an enemy to the truth.

The peace-making, conciliatory mind of Amadeus was staggered at these proceedings on the part of the Council. Such an outburst against the head of the Church he considered to be sacrilegious and invalid. Had Eugenius been guilty, as the Basilean Fathers assumed, they should have remembered that a decree of Theodoric the Arian, King of the Goths (when in A.D. 500 he had been asked to pronounce against Pope Symmachus), had declared that " God had willed that the

things of men should be judged by men ;
but that he whom He had chosen to fill
His See, the Most High alone would
judge ; and He willed that the successors
of St. Peter should owe their innocence
to Heaven alone, and commit their con-
science inviolate to the judgment of the
Most High."

But Amadeus's feelings, though shocked
at the irregularity of such proceedings,
were tempered with wariness. He was
careful not to commit himself to either
party, and with much tact he put forth a
protest, repudiating all that his ambassadors at Basle might have said or done
contrary to the obedience due by him to
the Catholic Church ; to which Church he
declared his determination ever to adhere
faithfully.

Upon receiving notice of the resolution
of his deposition, Pope Eugenius immediately annulled the Council.

Meanwhile, affairs were going on apace
at Basle. The only cardinal present was
the Cardinal of Arles. He was resolutely
determined upon giving Pope Eugenius

no opportunity whereby he might be returned to power. He feared that the Council might rescind its own action in suspending and deposing Eugenius; that he might be restored to favour and reinstated once more in the allegiance of his rebellious bishops. This was a contingency which was likely to occur as long as the papal chair was left vacant. If it could be filled by a substitute to whom would be accorded their homage as a lawful and reigning pope, the Cardinal's plans for the undoing of Eugenius would at last achieve success. He accordingly determined upon offering in nomination as Pope the name of Amadeus.

Upon the Council proceeding to elect a new Pope, the Cardinal of Arles had to bide his time, and to wait until a French candidate had been disposed of. The French party predominated at the Council, and through its influence the choice fell first on John, surnamed the Good, Count of Angoulême and Perigord, and son of Louis, Duke of Orleans, and Valentina of Milan.

After Duke Louis's assassination in 1407, Valentina, having found her beauty and her sorrow ineffectual in her appeal to King Charles VI. to obtain vengeance on her husband's murderers, withdrew to Blois. She died of grief the following year (1408), leaving the orphan John to the care of his elder brother, Charles, Duke of Orleans, himself aged only sixteen. In 1412, John was given by his brother to the English as a guaranty for the sum of one hundred thousand crowns, owed by the Duke for a force of English soldiers raised by him to support his cause against France. John remained a prisoner for more than thirty-two years, and his captivity was shared by his brother Charles, who was imprisoned in England from 1415 to 1440. The two brothers whiled away the hours of captivity by writing poetry, history, and moral philosophy. In order to regain his liberty John had to ransom himself by the payment of the one hundred thousand crowns. To raise this sum he was obliged to sell the County of Perigord, which was bought by

John of Brittany, Count of Limoges.
On his return to France he married Margaret, daughter of the Viscount de Rohan;
but he spent his life in seclusion, separated
alike from family and public affairs, absorbed in study and devout meditation.
His goodness and his retired, contemplative life gained for him many admirers;
and a majority of the Council of Basle
thought him a fit person to fill the papal
chair, and laid the offer before him. This
offer, however, was declined by John the
Good.

It would be more satisfactory to the
admirers of Duke Amadeus if they could
point to him as awaiting the result of this
turn in affairs with dignified equanimity
and calm indifference as to the personal
result. But such, unfortunately, was not
the case. Amadeus busied himself with
efforts to insure his own nomination.
Overtures were sent to several princes
with the idea of inviting their assistance
in this crisis. Among others he appealed
to his own son-in-law, the Duke of Milan.

The nationality of the electors to the

papacy shows that there was an attempt at giving an apparently equal representation to the nations sending delegates —France, Italy, Germany, and Spain. Savoy, however, secured a majority among the electors through an amusing technicality : it was insisted that Savoy should be considered as belonging to both France and Italy. There were twelve bishops among the electors : the Cardinal of Arles, the Bishop of Basle, and one Spanish and two French bishops ; the remaining seven bishops were Savoyards. The fact that a majority of these electors belonged to territories governed by the Duke of Savoy may have been the result of a fortuitous combination of circumstances ; but, so far as appearances go, it is difficult to maintain seriously that Amadeus, or, at any rate, his friends, had been trying to play fair.

The Council was induced by the Cardinal of Arles to place itself on record as maintaining the necessity of protection from the machinations of its enemies. On this account it was the duty of the

Council to elect as Pope one who, in the ordinary process of selection, would hardly have been suggested. It was necessary to pass out of the sphere of the ecclesiastics and the theologians, and to select one who could be efficacious in wielding the arm of the secular power. There was only one man, conspicuous for his piety and his devotion to the real interests of the Church, who was also rich and powerful enough to stand as a strong bulwark in defending her against the hostility of her foes.

It also has been claimed that the spite felt by Philip, Duke of Milan, against Pope Eugenius for his share in the wars in Italy, caused Philip to infatuate the Council at Basle into electing his father-in-law as Pope to displace Eugenius. This factor may have had some weight. However, after balloting four times, Amadeus, Duke of Savoy, as being the man for the times, was elected to fill the papal chair.

A deputation, comprising the most learned and influential Fathers of the

Council, waited upon the Duke to persuade him to accept the Papacy ; among
the number was Æneas Silvius Piccolomini, afterwards Pope Pius II.[1] In common with his other colleagues, he now
entreated Amadeus (for whom he always
expressed great admiration) to consent to
their proposal.   But Amadeus refused ;
he said that he had not renounced one
burden only to take up another; the de-

[1] Æneas Silvius Piccolomini, sprung from an ancient family
of Siena, was one of the leading humanists of the day. He
acted as secretary to Cardinal Capranica at the Council of
Basle. In a way that savoured more of craft and cunning
than of straightforwardness and constancy, he had the art of
ingratiating himself with each pope, in turn, whom that Council set up or deposed. Piccolomini also knew how to curry
favour with the Emperor Frederick III., and between imperial
power and papal patronage managed to attain by degrees to
the highest honours of the Church. Before being admitted to
holy orders his pen had run riot in a protest against papal authority as well as in a licentious novel entitled *A Story of two
Lovers* (Lucrezia e Eurialo). These writings he recanted in a
papal bull, dated 1463, as unworthy of one who had been
chosen as Christ's representative on earth. Having been sent
on a mission to Scotland by the Cardinal of Santa Croce, he was
present at the moment of the assassination of King James I.,
and took an active part in condemning the murderers. The
value of his historical writings may well atone for the failings
of his youthful pen, while his honourable record as Pope may
be more than enough to efface the memory of his early frail-
ties.

putation had to plead, to urge, even to threaten before the Duke showed any signs of yielding.   When the representation was made that resistance on his part was no less than an opposition to the will of God and would surely call down on him the wrath of the Most High, Amadeus submitted and accepted the dignity laid upon him.   Thus it was that Amadeus VIII., Duke of Savoy, became the last antipope.   This acquiescence has brought down upon him a mass of criticism which judged him very severely at the time, and has not yet been silenced.   His admirers see in his acceptance a sincere desire to heal the division in the Church; they dwell on his reluctance to accept the dignity, on the tears he shed on hearing that he had been elected to the post, on the sanctity of his life, on his renunciation of the throne and its glories; they maintain that he only yielded, at last, to pressure, and to the menace of peril incurred in rejecting a mission entrusted to him by God himself.

Another weighty argument in favour of

Amadeus's honesty is found in the fact that at the moment of his retirement, the schism in the Church was—chiefly through his means—in abeyance. He had protested against the sentence of condemnation that the Council was about to pass upon Eugenius; his protest, joined to that of the Duke of Burgundy, delayed the Pope's deposition for several years. Had Amadeus's aim been to become Pope, he would hardly have played the part of peacemaker with such zeal and success; nor would he have run counter to the wishes of the Council whose feelings he had ruffled rather than propitiated by his opposition, and by his insistence at such a moment for a higher place for his ambassadors than the one allotted to them by the Council.

But his accusers ascribe very different motives to him.[1] They say that the line of action pursued by him was designing

[1] Chief among these are : Flavio Biondo, Secretary of State to Pope Eugenius IV. ; Cibrario ; and Scarabelli in his learned dissertation entitled " Paralipomeni di storia piemontese dall' anno 1285 al 1617 " (*Archivio Storico italiano*, vol. xiii., Firenze, 1847).

and ambitious from beginning to end. They assert that he retired to Ripaille solely in the hope of eventually obtaining the Papacy ; that his refusal at first to accept the dignity was only part of a programme of assumed humility; and that the whole affair was prearranged between him and his son-in-law, the Duke of Milan, whose influence at the Council was all-powerful in gaining the election of the Duke of Savoy.

It is difficult to say positively which side of the controversy is in the right. Amadeus was a man with unbounded powers as an administrator; his talents for governing and directing were great and well known ; the love of ruling was strong in him, and he had retained authority when its externals had been discarded ; and it cannot be supposed that he was ignorant of his capabilities or willing to set them aside for ever.   In accepting the office of Pope he doubtless felt that his remarkable talents might bring about that concord in the Church which Eugenius IV. and his several Councils had failed to effect ; but

that he had this object in view when five
years previously he had chosen to retire
to the Hermitage of Ripaille is an hypothesis that one would not gladly accept.

The conclave that had elected Amadeus
VIII. to the Papacy was composed of men
of all nationalities and temperaments;
though this is not the place to dilate upon
the formalities which attended the session,
an incident described by Æneas Silvius Piccolomini [1] may be of interest, even if it fails
in the recital to arouse the laughter that it
provoked at the time of its occurrence.

The account given by Piccolomini deals
chiefly with the diet allowed during the
session; and after enlarging on the regulations, restrictions, and observances of the
Conclave he goes on to say : " Everyone
had to nourish himself on one variety
alone, whether of meat or of fish ; or if
neither one or the other was to his liking,
then on eggs and cheese. Besides, he
who chose meat had to content himself
with one quality only, so that he who had
beef could not also have mutton.   It was

[1] *Commentarii*

the same with fish ; he that had been helped
to lamprey could not also have eel. And if
anyone failed to observe this rule, he lost
his other helping at the door. The servants
not having observed this rule the first day,
and having brought to their masters a
most abundant and varied supper, as if
they had been at a wedding, were all de-
spoiled at the door, and but one kind of
dish was introduced for each member.
Among those who suffered from this de-
privation was the Archdeacon of Cracow.
Portions of mutton and of little birds had
been prepared for him, but the birds were
subtracted, though the servant at the door
begged that the more abundant portion
should be served to his master, hoping in
this way to have a helping of mutton for
himself instead of little birds. His master,
however, would have preferred the little
birds ; when he knew of the withdrawal,
he complained loudly and on all sides, declaring that never since he had been or-
dained priest had he spent a worse day.
And when he was entreated not to make
such an outcry, seeing that the same thing

had happened to the Cardinal (of Arles), 'Ah,' said he, 'you compare me to the Cardinal, a Frenchman, ascetic, not possessing a stomach, or, to say more truly, not even a man? I, unluckily for me, am placed next to him, and a transparent curtain enables me to see all that he does; and till now I have neither seen him eat nor drink. And what affects me more, he spends nights and days (although for us it is never day), without sleep, and he is always reading or occupied in business. His stomach is the last thing he cares for. I have nothing in common with him; I am a Pole; he is a Frenchman; he has a frigid stomach, while mine is burning; for him fasting is health, for me it is death. I, unless I eat much and sleep well, should faint; he is satisfied with everything. Let the Frenchmen fast; let the Poles eat.' These words caused universal merriment."

The work of election over, the next step was the installation of Amadeus into the new dignity laid upon him; the preliminaries took place at Ripaille.

The Pope-elect was unwilling to relin-

quish his beard.   He desired to be excused
from following another ecclesiastical custom : he did not wish to abandon his
secular name of Amadeus for a religious
name.   After gravely consulting upon
these serious questions, the envoys were
disposed to be indulgent for the time being and to refrain from compelling the
new Pope to use the razor.   But as to the
adoption of a new "name in religion"
they were as firm as adamant.   They made
this an indispensable condition before they
would consent to his inauguration.   These,
however, were trivial sources of annoyance to them, compared with a crushing
blow dealt to their expectations of financial advantage.

It was not an unpleasing prospect which
had opened out before them, that of becoming the members of the household of
a pope possessed of immense riches.   He
would be able to bestow substantial benefits with a lavish hand upon his favour-
ites.   But to their great disappointment
Amadeus showed no disposition to begin
distributing his vast fortune among his ec-

clesiastical adherents. On the contrary, he showed a disposition to regard his own possessions as merely held in trust by him ; he seemed to feel that they constituted a stewardship for which he should render strict account to his descendants. He was not inclined to expend for personal uses and ambitions what belonged to the House of Savoy. This feeling of responsibility to their princely House was almost a universal trait among the descendants of Humbert the White-handed ; to it, more than to anything else, is due the credit for the ever-advancing fortunes of this dynasty. It was perfectly natural and in the line of traditional policy handed down from remote ancestors, that Amadeus should firmly define his position and crush the expectations of the delegates from the Council. He said frankly: "You have abolished Annates[1]; what do you expect the Pope to live on ? I cannot consume my patrimony and disinherit my sons."

[1] A year's income of a vacant bishopric or other ecclesiastical benefice ; its estimated value for one year, paid as a tax to the Pope by the new incumbent.

The preliminary negotiations over, there followed the ceremony, which consisted in taking off the Duke's hermit's dress and arraying him in the spotless white papal robe; the pontifical ring was placed on his finger, and he was publicly recognised as Pope under the name, chosen by himself, of Felix V. His next act was to abdicate absolutely the sovereignty of his states. He appointed his son, Louis, as Duke in his stead, and named Louis's son, Amadeus (afterwards Amadeus IX.), Prince of Piedmont and Achaia; his second son, Philip, he made Count of Geneva. He then drew up his will and made provision for his beloved monastery of Ripaille. He instituted many rules and directions as to the Order of St. Maurice, which he designed to be a military-religious knighthood, possessed, too, of powers such as might belong to a privy council; he was most solicitous for its spiritual and temporal welfare. After clearly expressing his will that there should be one deacon and six knights (*milites*), he decrees that the deacon shall pay every year the

sum of 600 florins to provide for the preservation of the roofs of all the build-
ings, and to pay for the board and wages
of the servants of the Convent; while
each of the knights is to receive 200 florins for his board and clothing, and for
that, also, of the private servants. "As
endowment of the same *conventus mili-
taris* and of the knights and for the perpetual maintenance of their income the
above-named lord testator affirms to have
decreed and wills to give and assign forever and surely to the said Convent, 1000
florins of gold," and this sum was to be
forthcoming from certain places and things
judged expedient and seemly by the ex-
ecutors. The management of his hermitage was also regulated by Amadeus
before his departure; he named Claude de
Saix, lord of Rivoire, deacon in his stead;
then he set out for Basle, followed by a
numerous suite of noble and prelates.

The description of the newly elected
Pontiff's arrival and coronation at Basle
is given by Piccolomini in a letter to his
friend, "the Venerable and most learned

man, Master John of Segovia, most excellent theologian and orator of Our Most Holy Lord, Felix, at the Diet of Berry." The writer's desire to have his account of the proceedings perfect and exact is so urgent that it would be churlish not to allow him to relate in full scenes which he saw with his own eyes, and pageants in which he was himself a partaker :

" I imagine that through many voices the coronation of the Most High Pontiff will be known to thee and thy colleagues. But as I believe that many things will be misrepresented and incoherent I thought it well to testify to the truth with my letters and to give to you, thirsting for the truth, a reliable narration of all that was done. And, to be brief, I begin at once. It has rarely been heard that the Roman Pontiffs have been crowned at the General Councils ; thou knowest however, that Alexander was crowned at Pisa, and Martin at Constance ; but this coronation was as far above those as Felix is above them for nobility. Such is the judgment of those who witnessed this

one and the others.   I, therefore, and in
few words will speak of this one.   I will
not dilate on the election of this Pontiff
as brought about by the authority of this
Synod, of which I have already written
lengthily elsewhere.   I omit, too, the em-
bassy sent to him, and the consent that
he gave, of which things thou art well informed.

"I come to the coronation, which was
celebrated in this town of Basle on the
9th day of the Kalends of August.   Our
lord had made his entrance thirty days
previously, the eighth day of the Kalends
of July, about which it would be worth
while to dwell, but one cannot write of
everything at the same time.   In front of
the Cathedral is a spacious site, where
the popular sights are held.   A mound
was erected here ; and an altar placed on
its summit.   Above it were hung costly
draperies for protection against the sun
and the rain.   From this height one sur-
veys all the Square ; here ascended the
clergy, all the nobles, and the Pontiff
who was about to be crowned.   It was

calculated that two thousand men mounted
to this elevation.   The day before, Louis,
Duke of Savoy, son of the same Roman
Pontiff, had arrived, a man of benign expression, affable manners, just in council
and in mind.   He is of middle height;
his eyes are of the very brightest.   The
other son of the Most High Pontiff, Philip,
Count of Geneva, came with him; he is a
youth of exalted virtue, honourable and
honest in deeds and habits; in his company was Louis, Marquis of Saluces, of
whom thou couldst not say whether the
splendid presence or the eloquence was
more to be admired.   In the train of the
Duke of Savoy and of the Most High
Pontiff came, besides, the nobles of most
exalted rank in Savoy, all wishing to be
present at the coronation of their Prince.
So that there was indeed a goodly company of personages and of horses, reckoned
at four thousand.   From Germany came
the Marquis of Rothelin, beautiful in the
glory of his youth, with fair locks waving
in the wind; Conrad of Winsperg, He-
reditary Chamberlain of the Roman Em-

pire, a man old in years and in wisdom ;
the Count of Tierstein, who never had
his equal as youth and man, and who now
in his old age is incomparable.   There
came, besides, the orators of Strasbourg,
of Bern, of Fribourg, of Soleure, and all
the nobility of the neighbourhood.   Such
a multitude of people came together that
no one place could hold them all.   .   .   .
The town provided a thousand robust
youths in arms to prevent tumults ; of this
host, as admirable as they were formidable, part guarded the pavilion and part
the palace.   The roofs of the houses, the
windows, the trees, were all besieged by
men and women.   The Square, in the
meanwhile, was so full of people that
there would have been no place there for
a grain of mustard seed.

"At daybreak, in the presence of all
these masses, arrived the elected Felix ;
majestic in his appearance, in the dignity
of his white hairs, displaying to all a sin-
gularly decorous bearing.   His height, like
that of his sons, is medium ; for an old
man he is well made ; his skin and his

hair are white ; his speech is slow and
rare.   Preceding him came the mitred prelates and the neighbouring clergy.   He
took his seat in the most exalted place ;
the rest being seated, and general silence
being observed, the ceremonial began, in
which Felix showed himself so expert as
to need no assistance.   No one would
have thought that that Father, who for
forty years had been busied in secular negotiations, could ever have found time to
acquaint himself with ecclesiastical rites.
He himself corrected the mistakes of
others, and would not allow of the least
irregularity.   He celebrated his Mass,
singing and reading in so solemn a way
as not to be described, omitting nothing,
altering nothing.   The sight struck wonder into all, that old Father celebrating,
with his illustrious offspring assisting the
celebrant.   Like young olive branches
round about the altar, the two sons served,
diligent and attentive, as far as laymen
could.   All said that it might well be
affirmed that that felicitous one (Felix),
after having lived a praiseworthy secular

life, after having happily ruled his duchy
and educated his numerous offspring, had
been called by God to the control of the
Church universal.   Thou wouldst have
seen many weep for joy and bless the
Lord for having vouchsafed to them to
be present at such a sight; such as has
not been seen before or heard by anyone.
"It is customary in the midst of such solemn ceremonies to offer up supplications
in behalf of the Sovereign Pontiff.   The
eldest of the cardinal deacons begins them
and the secretaries and apostolical judges
take up the sacred song.   But on this day
the lawyers supplied the places of the
judges.   When, therefore, Louis, Cardinal
of Saint Sabine, a prelate of great repute,
and very learned in the ritual, began his
functions as cardinal deacon by intoning
the anthem, the secretaries and lawyers in
response gave utterance to such discord-
ant notes that everybody burst into laughter.   Some laughed even until the tears
ran down their cheeks, and for a week people spoke of nothing but this barbarous
singing.   Although many took this inci-

VIEW OF AIX-LES-BAINS IN THE EIGHTEENTH CENTURY.

dent in ill part and regarded it as an insult,
I, who was of the number, by no means felt
ashamed of my ignorance, for it is not given
to everyone to be perfectly acquainted
with church music. When therefore on
the following day it became necessary to
repeat the same anthem in the Church of
the Dominicans, I did not blush to do my
part as well as I was able.

"The Mass ended, and the Most High
Pontiff consecrated, the sacred tiara was
brought, glorious in its three gold crowns
all sparkling with gems. In the sight of
all this multitude and with deep emotion
Cardinal Louis—to whom the Synod had
entrusted this office, which should have
belonged to the Bishop of Ostia—about
now to gather the fruit of his labours,
placed on the happy head of Felix that
crown of immense value, judged by many
to be worth above thirty thousand ducats;
immediately the cry went up from all of
"Long live the Pope!" Plenary indul-
gences were then granted, which had never
before been given to that people.

"The ceremonial of the coronation

ended, the assembly left the pavilion, and the procession was formed, and all advanced on horseback. First of all marched the laymen and throngs of servants; second, came the distinguished families of the nobles; third, the nobles themselves and the knights; fourth, the barons, the counts and the marquises; fifth, came the young Duke, accompanied by his Councillors in robes of gold down to the ground. Each one of them endeavoured by a display of pomp to eclipse his neighbour. There were some decked in purple and gold; there were military dresses laden with silver and jewels, divers garments, divers ornaments, such as no one can even imagine.

"After these came the neighbouring clergy on foot, carring the relics of Saints, and a file of white-robed boys marched chanting. They were followed by a canopy of red and yellow around which stood the squires of honour, wearing red caps. Near to them would have been the naval prefects, had some of them been present, but in their stead were placed the Hermits of

Ripaille, who are called the Knights of St. Maurice; these are grave personages advanced in years, who have been comrades of Pope Felix both in his secular and religious life, and who showed by their dresses what his dress formerly had been; they were seemingly worthy of much reverence. Then came the priors with copes, and without mitres. Then followed the keepers of the chests and the advocates wearing their copes crosswise, a style of dressing much in keeping with their mode of singing. . . . The abbots followed next, and then the bishops, adorned with copes and mitres, and mounted on caparisoned horses. In this order we went before twelve horses, as white as snow, like those which Rhesus led to Troy, but covered with red clothing up to their necks, preceding a canopy.

" Directly after the bishops, among innumerable lights was borne the Body of our Lord Redeemer Jesus. The charge of conducting this was confided, as to a faithful sacristan, to John, Bishop of Strasbourg, a theologian of a knowledge as vast as it is useful. Then followed two cardinals and two bishops, those of Tursi, and of Vique, who held the post of deacons to the cardinals.   Last of all, desired by all eyes, came the Most High Pontiff under a canopy of of gold, with the triple crown on his head. Mounted on horseback, he advanced with slow paces, led by the Marquis of Rothelin and Conrad of Winsperg; he blessed the people as he came along.   After came the Treasurer, the clerks of the Chamber, and those who scattered money to the crowd, all in. fitting apparel.   The rear was formed of the orators of the Princes who happened to be there, and a confused multitude of folk.   Thus, as they passed through the out-of-the-way quarters of the town, the Jews, moved by new and fallacious hopes, drew forth the Mosaic law, which the new Pope praised while disapproving of their rite.   The procession repaired to the Convent of the Preachers (Dominicans), where the Brothers came forward with the Prior, and in front of the altar consigned to the Pope the keys of the Convent.   Hardly had they concluded a song of praise ere Felix, who was still fasting, withdrew, it being already the third hour after noon and nearer to supper than to dinner time.

" The following day all presented themselves at Mass ; this, and some other ceremonies, being ended, two pieces of silver money and one of gold were given to each prelate. And then the whole multitude was bidden to a feast, where there were no Orchian, Fannian, nor Licinian laws, nor indeed any sumptuary law whereby to fix the prices of the food or the quantity of the eatables. The supper (or was it the dinner? for there were doubts as to whether it was supper or dinner) was merry and sumptuous; by four o'clock more than 4000 men had supped. The cup-bearers were the two sons, the beautiful offspring of the Most High Pontiff ; the Marquis de Saluces directed the banquet. At three hours after midday they finished. At the hour of five they returned in the same order observed in going. The Pope after being accompanied to the Church of the Virgin, which is the chief one in Basle, entered the Palace by the

back way to rest. These things I will
that thou knowest concerning the coronation of our Most Holy Lord Felix the
Fifth ; thou canst now communicate them
to whom thou willest, and use thy diligence
to return as soon as possible to this Father
whom I esteem so highly, and to bring us
good news of your convent. Vale. From
Basle. The Ides of August, the year of
our Lord, 1440."

Felix V. was acknowledged as Pope by
England, France, Spain, Austria, Hungary, Bohemia, Bavaria, Switzerland, Savoy, Piedmont, and the Knights of the
Teutonic order. The rest of Christendom
acknowledged Eugenius IV., or else remained neutral ; among those not taking
sides were the Emperor of Germany and
the German Electors.

The indefatigable Cardinal of Arles
sought to strengthen the schism by still
further augmenting the influence exerted
by Amadeus through his alliances with the
great Powers of Europe. He proposed to
make the new Pope the father-in-law of the
Emperor of Germany. He accordingly

suggested to the Emperor Frederick the advisability of contracting a marriage with Margaret, the daughter of the Duke-Pope. She had been married to Louis of Anjou ; for some years she had been a widow. At first, this alliance appeared to strike the German Emperor favourably. When it became necessary, however, for him to commit himself, he toyed with the proposition. He did not see that it was to his interest to antagonise the Council, especially when it still included some powerful Electors of the Empire ; at the same time he was dismayed by the serious complications in prospect, if, in the progress of events, the schism became weaker. Then all persons, ecclesiastical or secular, who had committed themselves to its fortunes would suffer grievously in the general demoralisation. He hesitated to take a step which would alienate many dignitaries of Church and State throughout Europe. Still, he was afraid, just then, to decline the proffered honour of the hand of Margaret of Anjou, involving, as it did, an alliance with the Antipope and his Council of Basle.

Until Frederick could judge as to the amount of strength they were likely to gather, he could not afford to offend them. There was no course open to him but that of temporising. He took the matter under consideration, postponing any definite decision. He accepted an invitation to go to Basle. This gave the adherents of the new Pope great assurance for the fulfilment of their liveliest expectations, for they believed that the issue of personal negotiations between Frederick and Felix would lead to the success of their most audacious projects.

The entry of the German Emperor into Basle on November 11, 1442, was the signal for a triumphant demonstration by the dignitaries of the Council. They were discouraged, however, by the failure of Frederick to meet their expectations. They received him as an ally; he behaved merely as a neutral. He allowed nothing to betray him into breaking the strict reserve in which he enveloped himself. To the dismay of the schismatics he insisted on its being understood that he would not

visit Felix unless he could be excused
from making him obeisance as Pope. The
prelates determined to leave nothing un-
done which might help to impress the
mind of the Emperor during his interview
with Felix.   The Antipope was attired in
all the pomp and splendour of the Supreme
Pontiff.   He was attended by his eight
newly created Cardinals, together with
the Cardinal of Arles.   The papal retinue
moved majestically into the hall, preceded
by a cross-bearer.

The conference was a source of great
disappointment.   There were no productive results of any appreciable value.
Frederick maintained a respectful reserve.
The Fathers did not score a single point ;
and their affairs were not advanced one
step towards the goal of their ambitions.
The matrimonial alliance which had been
suggested by the Cardinal of Arles was
not furthered by the interview.   In fact
it was a source of disadvantage, in leading
Pope Felix to show his hand, and thus to
weaken the dignified attitude which a
claimant to papal honours should maintain

before the rulers of the state. Felix, finding all arguments unavailing to induce the Emperor to acknowledge him as the lawful incumbent of the papal throne, at last offered him a dowry of two hundred thousand gold ducats with his daughter Margaret, if he would pay the required allegiance. Even this, under the circumstances, proved of no value. After spending seven days at Basle, Frederick left, no more committed to the support of the schism than when he entered the city. Æneas Sylvius[1] says that as the Emperor was starting on his homeward journey, he remarked : " Before this, there have been popes who have bartered the honours of the Church ; Felix is ready to purchase them from anyone who can sell them."

The Emperor's declination of the marriage with the Pope's daughter was, after all, only a temporary reverse to the plotters at Basle. Frederick had disappointed. them by a negative attitude. Yet he had not espoused the cause of Felix's enemies. But the Emperor might be influenced if his

---

[1] Æneas Sylvius, *De Dictis Alfonsi*, lib. ii., 46.

Electors took a firm stand. The Electorate of the Holy Roman Empire was vacillating between the rival Popes. At first the Electors had formed a league in support of the old Pope Eugenius. This was promptly checked by the Emperor, who considered it a rash proceeding to commit the Electorate of the Empire to one side of the controversy. He did not feel that it would be expedient to antagonise the powerful supporters of the Savoyard Pope. Thereupon the German Electors abandoned Eugenius and veered around in favour of Pope Felix. The House of Savoy was too powerful, and there were too many among the rulers whose interests were associated with it by ties of kindred, for an Elector to be hasty in taking sides against Felix.

There were many suitors for the hand of the daughter of the Pope, for she had a dowry of two hundred thousand gold ducats. This was not the only marriage Felix had to offer. He also had a niece, whom he was ready to dower with a handsome marriage portion. Communications were opened between Felix and the Elector of Saxony in reference to the latter's son marrying the Pope's niece. This was in December, 1442, and, soon after, the Pope succeeded in espousing his daughter, Margaret, the widow of Louis of Anjou, to Count Louis, the Elector of the Palatinate. This was not so imposing an alliance as that which Felix previously had attempted to make with the Emperor of Germany. Still, in the ties which the Pope was able to form there was much to encourage him. All but two of the Electors of the German Empire were now enlisted in support of his schism. There was a high probability that the adherents of Felix would increase their strength so that they would be able by violence to wrest from Pope Eugenius his ecclesiastical dominion.

The contest between the papal rivals was no longer waged along the lines of ecclesiastical controversy laid down by the disputants at Basle. It had become a mere squabble for spoils on the part of the princes of Europe, with the battleground not in the Church, but in the

German Empire. The conflicting schemes of the German Electors were wrought in behalf of their individual interests, and utterly ignored the claims of Pope and Antipope, unless when a temporary espousal of either side was to be productive of direct political or personal advantage to an Elector. They were as ready to recognise Felix as they were Eugenius; one Pope was as acceptable to them as another. They were ready to commit themselves to only that line of conduct which would subserve their own interests. They were eager to ally themselves with the side which had the greater need of their help, if they could be sure of gaining ultimate triumph for that cause. In such a case they hoped to be able to dictate the best terms for themselves, and in the highest degree possible to augment their power and prestige.

The fortunes of Pope Felix seemed to offer to the German Electors the most encouraging indications that their services to his side would result in the most advantage to themselves. There was a fair chance of his winning in the end, but their assistance was so necessary that it was impossible for him to attain success independently of their efforts on his behalf. Hence the extent of his obligations to them would be all the greater. It was not essential to these schemes for their own aggrandisement that they should place him on the throne of universal dominion over the Church Catholic; he might fall far short of that and yet be in a position in which his power, controlled for the benefit of the German princes, could be still of tremendous benefit to them. They were for the Pope, whoever he might be, who could be of the most use to them.

The King of Arragon was willing to transport Felix V. to Rome and install him in the Chair of St. Peter by force. Amadeus wisely shrunk from this desperate enterprise. Afterwards this King of Arragon became reconciled to Eugenius IV.

At three successive Diets appeared the envoys of Basle and of Rome, of Felix and of Eugenius. Eugenius pronounced a deposition against the Archbishops of Co-

logne and of Treves, as adherents of Felix
V., the usurping pseudo-pope, but no one
thought of dispossessing these powerful
prelates, who were Electors of the Empire.
The Electorate at that time consisted of
seven princes, three ecclesiastical and four
secular. These were the Archbishops of
Cologne, Treves, and Mentz, the King of
Bohemia, the Duke of Saxony, the Mar-
grave of Brandenburg, and the Count
Palatine of the Rhine. The attitude of
the German Electors towards papal affairs
was so important a consideration with
Felix that he became indifferent to the
Council of Basle. The Fathers could
neither make nor mar his fortunes, and
as he was getting worn out by his life
at Basle, he was glad to leave the un-
wholesome atmosphere of the venerable
city. His sojourn there had been a sore
grievance to him. Serious inroads had
been made upon his health ; but the shock-
ing depletion of his purse had proved the
worst annoyance of all. The Council had
not once abated its constant drain upon
his resources for the defrayal of public

charges and individual expenses. He went to live at Lausanne in December, 1443. It was more peaceful and healthful than Basle, and gave him a much-needed relief from a troublesome Council which had become more expensive than useful to him.

While Pope Felix looked to Germany for the strength which would firmly intrench him in power over the Church, Pope Eugenius felt that in the play of Italian politics there would come round to him the opportunity which would enable him to regain the authority and influence which rightfully belonged to him as the lawfully constituted incumbent of the See of the Fisherman. As there were many contending interests among the scattered states of the peninsula, it would be in the line of good politics for all the Italian princes to restore the Papacy to its original prestige as a temporal power, in order to prevent any among themselves becoming too powerful at the expense of Rome, and thus a menace to their neighbours. Pope Eugenius built his hopes of eventual relief upon the certainty of the fact that the Italian princes could escape in no way from the necessity of committing to the Papal States the balance of power in Italy. They would be obliged to do this in self-defence, independently of any sentiments of friendliness or hostility towards the Roman Pontiff.

After having spent eight years in exile from his pontifical city of Rome, Pope Eugenius returned from Florence to the city by the Tiber.

The changing features of Italian conditions could not be without their effects upon the attitude of the German Emperor and Electors. These were maintaining what they called a strict neutrality ; but any toleration on their part of the claims of Felix, of course, constituted an imputation and a latent rebellion against the absolute and sole authority of the Pope at Rome. Any course they could take, short of the complete repudiation of the schism, was intolerable to Pope Eugenius. On the other hand, diplomatic negotiations, if carried forward in a way to arouse the cupidity of the Germans, might eventually prove the ruin of Felix.

There was only one man who was perfectly qualified to present acceptably the overtures of the Italian Papal Court to the German Emperor and his Electors. This man was the real author of the dissolution of the Council of Basle, of its gradual degradation in the estimation of Europe; he quietly drove Pope Felix to his abdication, and even added firmness and resolution to the obstinate and violent opposition of Pope Eugenius. This man was Æneas Sylvius Piccolomini.

It was Æneas who at Thonon saw Amadeus living in his hermitage, as he reports, " Magis voluptuosam quam pœnitentialem," a life of pleasure rather than of penance. Æneas became secretary to Pope Felix V.; afterwards he was secretary to the Emperor, then secretary to Felix's rival, Pope Eugenius, while Felix still was Antipope, and finally secretary to Pope Nicholas V. At last Æneas became Pope himself, under the title of Pius II.

Æneas was in many respects the cleverest man of his age. While he lacked the essential elements of greatness, yet he was a man of intellectual force, of varied culture, and far in advance of his period. Nevertheless, he was unable to emancipate himself from the low standards which guided the moral conduct of his associates. As a result he presents the sad spectacle of a man of the highest ability treacherously prostituting his faculties. He stood high in the confidence of the schismatics until he abandoned their camp for that of the German neutrals.

Æneas was one of the most prominent attendants at the rebellious Council of Basle. When Duke Amadeus of Savoy was elected as Pope, Æneas, as we have seen, was among the representatives of the Council sent to escort the Duke to Basle, where he was to be crowned with the papal tiara. Æneas was honoured by Pope Felix with the position of one of his secretaries. This gave the crafty Italian the opportunity of learning the internal affairs of this opposition Papacy. When

he found that very few continued to adhere to Pope Felix except those who were
devoid of ambition or ability, he determined to desert a sinking ship.   He went
to Germany to the neutrals.

Among the Germans Æneas met with
much success.   He was elevated by the
Emperor to the post of Imperial Poet, a
dignity which had been held by Petrarch.
He finally forsook his attitude of neutrality and became a warm adherent of Pope
Eugenius, whom he had formerly attacked
with fierce acrimony.

He so far brought about the repudiation of Felix and the restoration of the
German allegiance to Pope Eugenius that
at the death of the latter the schism was
utterly shattered and discredited.

For three years Felix lived in Basle;
in 1443, as we have seen, he removed to
Lausanne, from whence he often visited
Geneva.

Eugenius now, lest he should seem to
have his mind fixed upon nothing but
war, took a short respite from military
affairs and devoted himself to making

Nicholas Tolentunas a saint.   Tolentunas
was a monk of the Order of St. Augustine
who had had a number of miracles attri-
buted to him which had made him famous.
After that, Pope Eugenius expelled the
Canons Secular from the Lateran and
admitted only the Regulars.   Then, feeling that he had done his duty by things
spiritual for the time, he looked about for
a more congenial task.   He soon felt that
he had neglected the Florentines, to whom
he owed an old grudge.

Pope Eugenius accordingly determined
to bear down upon the unhappy town of
Florence, which had helped his enemies on
a previous occasion when he had been
sorely pressed.   He hit upon an ingenious
plan of campaign.   He had no doubt but
that if he attacked Florence with not only
his own forces, but also with those of his
allies, he could soon reduce the hapless
population to a properly humble and re-
pentant state of mind.

Unfortunately for Pope Eugenius, all
these beneficent designs were frustrated
by his death.   Still the love for war had

been developed to so great a degree in the
Pope that, besides his Italian campaigns,
he instigated the Dauphin, son of King
Charles of France, to go with a great body
of horse against the forces of Basle.   He
did so and routed the adherents of the
Council.

Their cause was now so hopeless that
the Fathers at Basle yielded to the friendly
urgency of the Kings of France and of
England.   They were abandoned also by
the Emperor of Germany, who threatened to dissolve the Council.

Felix was still living in Lausanne when
Eugenius IV. died in 1447.

The Conclave at Rome chose as Eugenius's successor, Thomas di Sarzana, who,
as Pope Nicholas V., was one of the most
learned pontiffs who ever filled the Chair
of St. Peter.   His election gave rise to
the universal hope that peace would be
restored, and that the scandal of two
Popes would be removed.[1]   The qualifi-
cations of the new Pope were such as to

[1] At the coronation of Pope Nicholas V., Æneas Sylvius
Piccolomini officiated as cross-bearer.

make Felix realise that his services in
that capacity were no longer required, and
that his mission would be better fulfilled
by the renunciation of a post which, in
his heart, he must have recognised was
not the place for him. He consequently
empowered his son, Duke Louis, to enlist
the good offices of Charles VII., King of
France, to settle the differences between
him and his rival. The matter was concluded in 1449, when Felix V., at a council
convoked by him at Lausanne, declared
" that, for the peace of the Church
and to make an end of the schism, he
renounced the Papacy." His act of self-
denial (for such it undoubtedly was) met
with a proper reward. He was named
Bishop of Sabina, Cardinal Legate and
Perpetual Vicar of the Holy See in all
the states subject to " Casa Savoia," and
in Switzerland and Germany; he was to
rank immediately after the Pope; he was
not to be spoken of as the " Antipope,"
but as " the former Pope Felix V." [1]; and

[1] Predari, *Storia politica, civile, militare della dinastia de
Savoia dalle prime origini a Vittorio Emmanuele II.* (Torino,

(a matter of primary importance to him and to his followers) the nominations and ordinations he had made during the nine years of his pontificate were to be recognised as valid ; his acts, in union with those of the Council of Basle, were to hold good; while the excommunications uttered against him by the late Pope Eugenius IV. were all declared null and void. At the same time, Felix was to exercise the same courtesies towards Nicholas and the Holy See ; he was, together with the Council of Basle, to acknowledge Nicholas V. as the one and true Pontiff; he was to recognise the acts passed by him and the late Eugenius as lawful; and he was to remove all the anathemas and excommunications uttered in the past. On retiring from the Papacy, Felix received certain concessions in regard to ecclesiastical appointments which placed the Church of Savoy on a footing of independence very remarkable in that age.

1869), vol. i., p. 255, foot-note : '' In all the bulls of Nicholas V., Amadeus is always called, ' Felicem Papam Quintum tunc in sua obedientia nominatione.' ''

There was universal rejoicing throughout the whole of Christendom at this
happy termination of a strife, unworthy
alike of those who took part in it and of
the cause for which it was undertaken.
The popular sentiment found expression
in a line which declared :

" Lux fulsit mundo, cessit Felix Nicolao,"

which may be rendered rudely :

The world was once more bathed in light,
When Felix to Nich'las restored his right.

A whimsical conceit has made of this
memorial verse a cryptogram. By changing the *s* of *fulsit* into an *x*, and adding
together the Roman numerals contained
in the line, the year of the Antipope's abdication, 1449, may be formed.

The outburst of good feeling, however,
was occasionally disturbed by a few recal-
citrants who refused to be reconciled.
For instance, Poggio Bracciolini, one of
the scholars at the Court of Pope Nicholas V., pays his respects in no uncertain
tones to the ex-Pope Felix V., who was

then living in retirement at Ripaille. He calls him "another Cerberus," "a high priest of malignity," "a perverter of the faith and foe to true religion," "a golden calf," "a rapacious wolf," and "a roaring lion." He waxes furious as he recalls the turpitude of the Council of Basle which elected this Antipope. It is "that sink of iniquity, the Synagogue of Basle," "a monstrous birth," "conventicle of reprobates," "riotous band of debauched men," "apostates, libertines, ruffians, deserters, men convicted of the most shameful crimes, blasphemers, rebels against God."

Writers unfriendly to Amadeus allege that he did not renounce the tiara voluntarily. According to Monod, his tenacity in retaining his dignity was due to the encouragement of Guilliaume Bolomier, a man who had raised himself by his talents from a humble condition to that of Chancellor of Savoy. He was absolutely in Duke Amadeus's confidence; he was employed by him in all missions and embassies of an important or confidential nature, and became also his private secretary.

But he paid dear for the fortune which had raised him to such heights. Duke Louis disliked him for the influence he had over his father, and for the way in which that influence was directed in connection with the Papacy. The Piedmontese nobles hated him for his arrogance and insolence towards them, and they determined to work his downfall. They succeeded so well in their endeavours that Duke Louis consented to his condemnation, and signed the warrant for his decapitation. This, however, was commuted to what was considered a milder form of punishment; the unfortunate man was taken from his prison in the Castle of Chillon, placed in a boat, and thrown by the hangman into the Lake of Geneva with a stone tied round his neck.

Amadeus's detractors maintain that he only renounced the Papacy for the advantages that he gained by so doing; but the more likely hypothesis is that he desired the welfare of the Church and rejoiced in the knowledge that this was achieved by his self-abnegation. He retired at once to his beloved hermitage at Ripaille, where he lived in peace, surrounded by the Knights of St. Maurice and wholly given over to religion. In January, 1451, he died at Geneva, a town for which he had always had a great affection, and where, up to the last, he exercised the office of Bishop. " He finished his days in miracles and holiness, having reigned —taking together his duchy and his pontificate—about forty years; and he rendered his peace to the Holy Church, his duchy to Monseigneur Louis, his only son,[1] his body to the earth, and his soul to God the Creator."[2] His body was interred at Ripaille, but the tomb was broken into by the insurgents of Bern, in 1538, in seeking treasure. His bones were afterwards collected by Emmanuel Philibert I., and laid in the cathedral at Turin; they now rest in the chapel of St. Sudario in Turin, where King Charles Albert erected a fine mausoleum over them. A fine monument to Amadeus

[1] His other son, Philip, Count of Geneva, had died in 1444.
[2] Paradin, *Chronique de Savoye*, p. 333, Lyon, 1552.

VIII. is still shown in the cathedral at Lausanne.

The character of Amadeus VIII. is not easy to fathom. The deeper one dives into the intricacies of his story the harder it becomes to form an impartial judgment upon a mind that blended so strangely the things of earth and of heaven. Ambition sounded the key-note of his nature ; that element entered largely into his thoughts and actions. And though this theory is not confirmed by his five years' retirement and seclusion at Ripaille, it reasserts itself on the evidence of the last two years of his Papacy, which were spent in piteously clutching at the shadow when the substance of the Keys was slipping from his grasp, when he still clung to a position that his dignity neither as Pope nor Prince could permit him to occupy.

But who again can say that ambition was the sole motive of his action ? The idea of becoming Pope of Rome to one who had already renounced the Dukedom of Savoy seems so original and quaint, that the excuse of ambition hardly sanctions it, nor does it satisfactorily explain the Duke's conduct. The legend that such a destiny had been foretold to him by an astrologer and that the prophecy had taken hold of his imagination seems again hardly sufficient to warrant one's acceptance of this surmise; so the enigma remains yet unravelled, and the key of the mystery must be found ere the riddle can be read aright, and the problem fairly solved.

That Amadeus acted uprightly in his capacity of Pope has been universally admitted; his appointments to the Church's benefices (he created in all twenty-five Cardinals) were made according to merit, never with a view to favour his relatives; to quote Monod's words: " He never mixed the ecclesiastical purple, dyed with the Blood of Christ, with his own, although he had many grandchildren, his son Louis's sons; but he willed that it [the Cardinalate] should be the reward of merit, not of kinship." [1]

One account of his behaviour to the Emperor Frederick III. shows a high nobility of mind and disdain for money-hunters.

[1] Monod, *op. cit.*, p. 179.

The Emperor was under the delusion that
Amadeus VIII. was enormously rich ; with
a view to possessing himself of some of
this wealth, he reflected that he might take
to wife one of the Duke's daughters, provided only that her father would give her
a large dowry.   With this intention Frederick repaired to Basle, and there had a
secret colloquy with the papal Duke. " But
when Amadeus perceived that it was not
so much the connexion that was sought
after as the money (and notwithstanding
that the Fathers counselled otherwise), he
cut short all negotiations." [1]   According
to this account Frederick was far from
pleased at having thus deluded himself.

Although Amadeus abundantly showed
the possession of a varied genius, and a
sincere and indulgent heart, always open
to the finest sentiments of humanity, yet
his rule as Pope was not as useful as he
might have made it.   While his own acts
as Supreme Pontiff were upright and honourable, his pontificate was not advantage-
ous to the world at large.   The clergy

[1] Monod, *op. cit.*, p. 181.

under his rule grew insolent, while the contempt entertained for them by the laity became intensified. Amadeus's own renown as a leader and administrator waxed ever fainter. The verdict of a modern writer upon the Hermit-Duke is that " he finished without glory a life gloriously begun." [1]

But a less harsh sentence and a pleasanter to carry away in one's memory of a prince who, whatever his faults may have been, was undeniably a great man, is to be found on the monument erected to him by his descendant, the Cardinal Prince Maurice of Savoy, in the church of Carignan, where with pride and reverence the virtues of " the mighty dead " are recounted as follows :

" Seventh of the name, thirteenth in the succession, first in the Dukedom,
  Three times great.

In puerile innocence, in youthful wedlock, in senile celibacy,
  Three times pious.

With his sons, with his subjects, with his neighbours,
  Three times peaceful.

[1] Scarabelli, *op. cit.*

In the Dukedom, in the Pontificate, in the
    Legation,
> Three times just.

By acclamation of his own, of strangers, and
    of Councils,
> Three times Solomon.

In the worship at the Hermitage, in the exalted-
ness from the Hermitage, in the return to the
Hermitage,
> Three times felicitous.

In his life, in his death, in his miracles,
> Three times holy."

ARMS OF AMADEUS VIII. AS POPE FELIX V.

CHAPTER II

THE HOME-SURROUNDINGS OF THE HOUSE
OF SAVOY IN THE FIFTEENTH CENTURY.
TASTES, FASHIONS, AND PERSONALTIES.
INVENTORIES OF THE OBJECTS CONTAINED
IN THE DUCAL PALACES OF TURIN, CHAM-
BÉRY, AND PONT D'AIN AT THE CLOSE
OF THE FIFTEENTH CENTURY

IT is useless to attempt to portray the history of any people without allud-ing to their tastes, their habits, their fashions, and their intellectual pursuits. There is no intention in this chapter to discuss the art of this period of Savoyard history. Such a dissertation would be altogether beyond the aim of the present work, but some account of the personal tastes and fashions of the dukes and duch-esses of Savoy may not be out of place at this point of their story. The condition in which Savoy found itself at the mid-

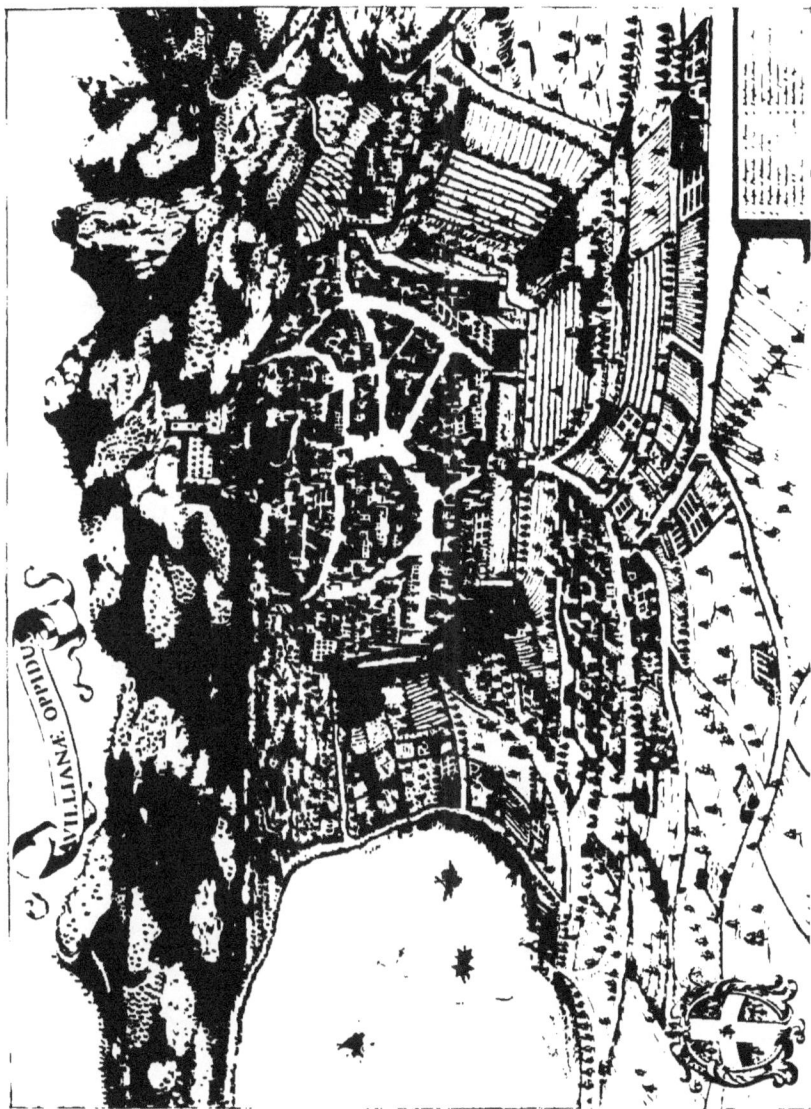

VILLIANÆ OPPIDU

VIEW OF AVIGLIANO.

dle of the fifteenth century was one of
prosperity and culture. This was due in
a great measure to the wisdom and administration of Amadeus VIII., nineteenth
Count and first Duke of Savoy.

The position held in Europe by the
Duke as arbitrator in the quarrels of his
neighbours, and as their referee in all
questions requiring acumen, had brought
to his Court a number of ambassadors and
statesmen, who came for counsel and advice. They, in their turn, brought a stir
and an animation which had its effect in
stimulating trade, in enlarging the ideas,
and raising the tastes of all classes throughout the country. The brilliancy of Duke
Amadeus's Court gave an encouragement
to art as well as to home and foreign industries. The magnificence with which
the princes of Savoy, at this epoch, surrounded themselves, in their private as
well as in their public life, proved of two-
fold advantage to their Court. It gave an
incentive to trade and manufacture that
brought abiding good to Savoy; it also
served as an impetus to commerce in such

a way as to advance social development by several centuries.

The wealth then existing in the duchy is revealed in the inventories which have come down to us. The minuteness of these records gives us an insight into the luxury and fashions, the tastes and the entertainments indulged in by the princes and princesses of the House of Savoy. A long list exists of the literary and artistic treasures contained in the three ducal residences of Turin, Chambéry, and Pont d'Ain. This catalogue enumerates and describes no less than one thousand, six hundred and thirty different items: three hundred books, manuscripts, and codices; three hundred jewels, pieces of plate, and valuables appertaining to the Treasury; five hundred pieces of tapestry; three hundred hangings, draperies, and utensils for the services and decoration of the Church; two hundred pieces of armour, of ironwork, and of furniture.

It is impossible not to be impressed by the costliness of these possessions: the wonderful miniature-painting in most of

the codices ; the exquisite workmanship
in the design and execution in the jewellery ; the value and variety of the stuffs ;
the tapestries displaying the records of past
and present history with every detail as
to beauty of colour and pattern carried out
in the elaboration of their threads ; the
furniture and other treasures betokening
unrivalled sumptuousness, and bespeaking
for the House of Savoy a splendour the
knowledge of which has but lately come
to light, and displays the luxury and taste
existing in Savoy four hundred years ago.
Duke Amadeus's Court became a rallying
point for artists from every land.   During
his reign a large influx of artificers, painters, sculptors, goldsmiths, embroiderers,
musicians, and miniature-painters found
favour and occupation in Savoy.

The same order of things was continued
under the weak and vain Lodovico, or
Louis, Amadeus's son and successor. This
condition may be said to have reached the
meridian of its prosperity in that reign, for
to Louis's love of display was added that
of his wife, Anna of Cyprus. Her Oriental

nature delighted even more than that of
her husband in all the luxury and magnificence that wealth and self-indulgence could
supply. " Under Duke Louis, whose vanity and weakness are well known," says a
modern writer, " the decorative arts and
industries received a still greater impetus
from the splendour of the Court, from the
immoderate luxury, from the extravagant
revellings in gold and gems, from the
prodigality of the gifts and the wasteful-
ness of every kind, into which the lovely
and capricious Anna of Cyprus dragged
her feeble consort. The unfortunate,
steadily declining condition of the ducal
finances availed in no way to check the
enormous purchases of precious cloths of
gold and of silver, of silks, of jewels, and
of the thousand other costly articles which
fed the luxury of the Court. This extravagance, in its turn, nourished and in-
creased art and industry.[1]

To give the precedence to jewels, gifts,
and clothes would cast a reflection on the

[1] P. Vayra, " Le lettere e le arti alla Corta di Savoia nel
secolo XV.," *Misc. di Storia It.*, T. xxxii., p. 20.

literary treasures owned by the dukes of
Savoy. We will simply follow in the steps
of those who drew up the inventory, and
lead off with the books and manuscripts,
even if the chronological order is not always strictly maintained. The first inventory, which was made by "Messieurs
Amyé de challes maistre d'oustel de mon
tres redoubté seigneur Monseigneur le duc
de sauoye et Jehan vulliod trésorier de
sauoye" [Messrs. Amyé de Challes, Stew-
ard of my very redoubtable lord, Monsignor the Duke of Savoy, and Jehan (John)
Vulliod, Treasurer of Savoy], the 25th of
October, the year of grace 1498, opens
with a list of the books to be found at that
period at the Castle of Chambéry, these
books being for the most part kept in
cases or coffers. These coffers are covered either with cloth or leather, the cloth
being generally red, the leather black, and
they are barred and bolted in a way that
hints of more security for the books than
of facility of access to the reader. The
cases, too, are generally lined. All be-
tokens a care for the books that has

availed to preserve many of them intact to the present day. Many of them are of great value ; many deal with religious subjects. The exactness with which they are catalogued shows with what faithfulness the "maistre d'oustel" and the "trésorier" carried out their work. No detail is omitted, and the condition of the book receives as much notice as its authorship and nomenclature. Thus No. 5, for instance, is spoken of as follows : "Vng aultre gros liure en parchemin, escript à la main, traictant de la disputacion de sainct paul contre symon l'enchanteur, commencant á la grosse lectre : Quant sainct *paul*, couuert de paul et de cuyr à vng meschant fermail de peau et locton " [Another great book on parchment, written by hand, treating of the disputation of St. Paul against Simon the Magician, beginning with the capital letter (probably illuminated) : "When St. Paul," covered with skin and with leather, with a faulty clasp of leather and *locton*]. This work, of which a manuscript copy exists in the Bibliothèque Nationale, of

Paris, treats of a legend relating to St.
Paul, beginning, " Quant St. Paul fu
venus à Rome tuit li juif vindrint à lui," etc.
[When St. Paul came to Rome all the Jews
came to (see) him, etc.]. The copy at Paris
dates from the end of the thirteenth century, and at the conclusion the authorship is
ascribed to Marcellus. The " faulty clasp "
evidently points to its being out of repair,
or in some way wanting in the duties required of it. The subjects of many of the
books are interesting as showing the occupations of the day, the habits of the counts
of Savoy in those times, and the bent of
their minds. Thus we come upon "vng
petit liure de parchemin, escript, à la main,
traictant du jeu de l'eschacquier appellé
doctrine, illuminé d'or et d'aczur, folliagé
tout a l'entour de la première margine
commencant : Cy commence, couuert de
post et de vellours déciré a quatre fer-
meaulx à boucles d'argent douré, et deux
agullectes de ruban ou il y a trois fers
d'argent douré " [A little parchment
book, written by hand, treating of the
game of chess or checkers called *doctrine*,

illuminated with gold and azure, foliated all round the first margin, beginning : " Here begins," covered (in) boards with torn velvet, with four clasps of silver gilt and two ribbon straps, with three nails or studs of silver gilt].   Chess, then, was evidently a pastime in the House of Savoy ; and the description of this torn, used work on the subject shows that the game was one frequently indulged in, the matter well studied, and the volume often in the hands of the combatants.   Can the damaged condition of this little work be explained in any way ?   Can it be that the sting and smart of a triumphant "checkmate" would have so stirred the choler of the defeated player that no reprisals could be found, save those of flinging at the head of the victor the little tome, whose counsels had been powerless to avert defeat ?

Another book shows that the taste of that day was not unlike our own, and that *The Romaunt of the Round Table* and *The Romaunt of the Rose* were read and studied then as now.   The copy of the latter in the Duke's collection was by

William of Lorris; and the very copy
here mentioned exists to this day in the
Biblioteca Nazionale of Turin. This
is followed again by volumes on sacred
subjects; then come works of Seneca and
translations from the French. After nine-
teen books have been named and described, the contents of the first "couffre"
are concluded, and those of the second
are catalogued.

This collection, well bolted and barred
within "vng aultre couffre couuert de
cuyr noir" [another coffer covered with
black leather], contains a famous manuscript of the date of 1294, known as the
Bible historiale, of which "la première
histoire est de dieu le père aucques les
quatre euuangelistes, commençant : Pour
ce que les dyables," etc. [the first history
is of God the Father also the four evan-
gelists, beginning : "In order that the
devils," etc.]. It is bound in boards covered with crimson velvet, in which are
nine nails in the shape of St. Maurice's
cross ; it has two clasps fastened with
green silk, and the clasps and the nails

are all silver-gilt. A very fine Codex
which tallies with this description is to be
found at the National Library at Turin,
and is looked upon as being the copy in
question. No less than sixteen "couf-
fres" are catalogued in turn, all covered
either with red cloth or black leather,
many of them lined, and all carefully
guarded with iron bars and locks. Contained in these various strongholds are to
be found works by Dante; Froissart;
The Romance of Fier-à-bras; the poems
of Charles, Duke of Orleans, written during his captivity in England; *The Hundred Tales* of Boccaccio; the writings of
Boethius; Cicero; the Fathers of the
Church; the *Mirouer du Monde* [" Mirror
of the World," a book much in vogue at
that epoch]; works on medicine; on the
preservation of health; the *Lives of Illustrious Men,* by Cornelius Nepos; works
on the diseases of horses, and their treat-
ment; others concerning precious stones;
others concerning the siege and fall of
Troy; of tournaments and the art of
chivalry; plays, both sacred and profane;

and other works of rare editions and great value, bringing the collection up to about three hundred volumes.

The list of books being concluded, the inventory proceeds with articles of a more housewifely nature under the heading of " La Tappisserie," hangings and draperies decorated with clouds, angels, scrolls, leaves, and flowers.   One coverlet is thus described : " Vng aultre banchie [literally, covering for a bench] bleu fait a nueez, dessus a quatre anges tenant escrips en leurs mains " [another blue coverlet with clouds, on which are angels holding scrolls in their hands].   Others again are ornamented with the arms of Savoy, together with those of the princesses who married into the ducal house.   We find the Savoy motto, " F. E. R. T.," surrounded with the love-knots or bows ("lacz, lacci") which give it so decorative an effect.   Griffins, wild animals, scenes from hunting and rural life, are all in fantastic designs, displaying the taste and execution of the different crafts employed in the manufacture of these tapestries.

Together with " La Tappisserie " comes a list of linen of every sort and condition : embroidered, plain, painted, with trimmings and without, adapted for every variety of purpose.   Many pouches, bags, and purses are also described ; a box wherein is contained a large hat of grey felt "a vn soleil dessus fait de petites perles " [has a sun upon it made of little pearls].   There are banners and fly-wisps —an Eastern importation, which from having been a piece of household furniture was afterwards used in religious services.

Numerous also are the hangings and curtains for church purposes.   One is " vng drap de vellours gris pour vng parement d'oustel, brodé dessus de fil d'or et soye, la vie de sainct pierre et sainct pol, armoyé aux quatre coinetz de crois blanches tout a l'entour de lacz de sauoye, et Fert, doublé de toyle rouge " [an altar-cloth of grey velvet, embroidered in gold thread and silk, with the lives of St. Peter and St. Paul emblazoned at the four corners, with white crosses round Savoy knots, and F. E. R. T., lined with red cloth].

Another is "vng aultre grant drap de vellours verd brodé dessus la vie de sainct
Jehan baptiste a grans personnages d'or
et soye, armoyés au dessus et aux coustés
tout au long de petites croix blanches et
des armes de Bourgongne my parties et
doublé de toyle noyre" [another great
cloth of green velvet with the life of St.
John the Baptist embroidered on it, with
great figures in gold and silk emblazoned
upon it (or above), and all along the sides
little white crosses, and the arms of Burgundy in the middle, and lined with black
cloth].

Stuffs in damask, in silk, in linen, in
cloth of gold, in velvet, in satin, in serge,
and in other materials, of every colour,
with patterns and designs innumerable,
go to make up a collection which must
have been complete in its way, and of
immense value at that date. Hunting and
forest scenes were evidently favourite subjects with the ducal family of Savoy, and
very effective and beautiful many of them
must have been. Such, for instance, as:
" Deux pans de soye blanche ouuré a

ouurage de napples a folliages de brodeure d'or et soye verde a vng jardin verd,
trois fames et vng homme dedans trois
arbres, a celluy du mylieu de la croix
blanche pendue et tout de brodeure"
[two panels of white silk embroidered
with Naples work with foliage in gold
and green silk, a green garden with
three women and a man within, three
trees, on the middle one a white cross
hanging, and all embroidered]. Or take
again : " Vng aultre grant tappis de ver-
dure a forestz a grant personnaiges,
hommes et femmes à chevaulx chassans
de hors" [Another great hanging of a
green forest with great figures of men
and women on horseback bear-hunting].
This "chasse de hors" being the chase
of the bear (*ours*), not "out of doors," as
might at first strike one's imagination.

A lengthy list is reserved for the bed-
hangings, together with their adornments
and the materials of which they are made.
Very beautiful must have been these
"ciels" and "douciels" (canopies and dos-
sals) with much minute detail worked in

figures, foliage, beasts (including uni-
corns), birds, such as hawks, peacocks,
etc., scrolls, inscriptions, and heraldic devices.

The tricolour of red, white, and green
is often mentioned, and it is interesting to
notice how constantly the mixture of these
colours—which in after times were to become the national colours of Italy—were
introduced in the stuffs, jewellery, and
decorations of the ducal House of Savoy
hundreds of years ago. A necklace given
to Margaret of Savoy, daughter of Amadeus VIII., on the occasion of her (second)
marriage with Louis, Duke of Bavaria, is
said to have weighed one mark, six ounces,
and nine pennies, and to have been enamelled in green, white, and red. These
colours again made their appearance in a
coverlet which is thus described : " Vne
couuerte de litière de velours cramoysi
doublé d'Vng drap de turquie de soye
Rouge, ouuré ladite doubleure de ladite
soye et Rozes d'or, frengé de soye blanche,
verde et rouge " [a bed-cover of crimson
velvet, lined with a Turkish cloth of red

silk, the said lining of the said silk being embroidered, and with gold roses, and fringed with silk, white, green, and red]. On other stuffs the arms of Yolande of France, the arms of Montferrat, of Bourbon, of Burgundy, of Bresse, of Cyprus (the last in honour of Anna of Lusignan), are in turn embroidered with those of Savoy. By the richness and variety of their quarterings they must have greatly enhanced the decorative effect of these hangings.

Even the mattresses are thought of and their quality mentioned in this comprehensive list. The first one spoken of is, however, of a humble order, and only "vng grant matrat de cocton fait de fustenne carrelli" [a great mattress of cotton made of (or covered with) plaid fustian]. The next is more imposing, being "vng aultre mactrat de velours cramoysi grant doublé de taffetas gris déciré ledit taffetas" [another great mattress of crimson velvet lined with grey silk, the said silk being torn]. Think of a crimson velvet mattress! No wonder that the light grey silk lining should get torn in the daily process of turning, if such liberties could be taken with mattresses of that value !

The mattresses disposed of, lengthy mention is made of articles for church use. Then the tale begins again of linen and household properties, sheets of all sizes and qualities, table-cloths, napkins, cushions, pillow-cases (these latter made of silk, nay, even of velvet as well as of linen), and an unlimited amount of tapestry, on some of which is worked the portrait of Du Guesclin, and on some that of " mistère sainct george."

The armoury is also mentioned. The list here is a short one, of no special artistic or historic interest, though so exact is it that not even an old and bad pair of bellows "for blowing the fire " is omitted.

To enumerate all the objects recorded in these inventories would prove wearisome, for several pages follow, filled only with articles for the Duke's private chapel, and then all the minutiæ of goods contained in his palaces at Chambéry, Turin, and Pont d'Ain. But an occasional object

now and again attracts attention and re-
quires a special notice, as in the case of
" Maistre Jehan's " room, which may be
taken as a specimen of a bachelor's apartment with a certain claim to comfort, thus :
" En la chambre de maistre Jehan " (who
Maistre Jehan may be does not transpire,
but he may have been one of the gentlemen who drew up the inventory and who
is spoken of as " Maistre Jehan Vulliod,"
Treasurer of Savoy) " vng lit moyen garny
de cussin, trois couuerte barrées, vng ciel
de toille blanche et les quatre pendans,
vne table de noyer, deux trecteux, trois
bancs de chesne tant, grans que petis,
troys grans escabelles et vne petite, vng
meschant buffet de sappin, deux trellis a
mettre sus le lit " [a medium-sized bed
furnished with pillows, three cross-barred
coverlets, a canopy of white cloth and the
four hangings, a table of chestnut, two
trestles, three oaken benches, large and
small, three large stools and one small
one, a poor buffet of pine, two trellised
gratings to put over the bed]. The use
of these trellised gratings on the beds was

to prevent the dogs from getting on them and damaging the rich coverlets at that time so much in use. The footnote which gives this explanation offers almost an apology for the need of such things, bidding us make allowance for the age in which such practices were in use, and excusing the rough habits of the day.

One curious item among a heap of tables, old bits of iron, and odds and ends of every sort, is one for some wood for "le lit de mal repos" [the bed of ill repose], a weird and pathetic wording for the bed wherein all must some day seek rest, and which is more commonly spoken of as a coffin.

To show how exact this inventory is, it suffices to take note of "vne meschante nappe toute déciree que ne vault riens et de trous dedans, aultres nappes à fillez noirs qui ne valent riens" [a faulty table-cloth, all torn, which is worth nothing, with holes in it, and others with black netting, which are worth nothing]. The inventory also makes mention of the entire apparatus for a bath, of warming-pans, and of all the

utensils needed for domestic life. It fur-
nishes us with the proof that life in those
days was not so unlike our own, and that
the comforts, cleanliness, and luxury which
we are apt to consider as peculiar to our-
selves were known and practised in Savoy
four centuries ago.

It may be that a glance at the " Etrennes " or New Year's gifts, made by the different dukes and duchesses, will be of
interest in serving to show the fashions of
that day, and the costliness of the presents
given by these personages to the members
of their family, their household, and de-
pendents at the beginning of each year.
The inventory from which the following
extracts are taken bears the date of 1445,
when Louis, son of Amadeus VIII., and
his wife, Anna of Cyprus, were reigning
in Savoy. An offering made by Duchess
Anna to the Pope shows how even then
the mosquitoes were as troublesome as to-
day, and how different remedies were tried
in order to escape from so persistent an
evil. The Duchess sends a gift to the
Holy Father in the shape of a candle-

stick of gold made to represent a labourer, wherein to hold some " birds of Cyprus," these "birds" being composed of some grain or powder, burnt as pastilles to destroy, or at least stupefy, the mosquitoes. The gift is thus described in the inventory : " Pour j chandelier dor a tenir oysellons de Cypres, fait a fasson dung gaigneur pesant xj onces iiij deniers d'or ; lequel ma Damme donna a nostre tressaint Pere pour bonne estrayne ledit jour de lan ; (encluz xxvj ecus pour la fasson cxjiij escuz et demie)" [for a gold candlestick to hold birds of Cyprus, made in the fashion of a labourer, weighing eleven ounces four deniers of gold, which my Lady gave to our most holy Father for a good gift the said New Year's Day, one hundred and fourteen crowns and a half, including twenty-six crowns for the making].

The Duke's present to his Holiness consisted of a gold salt-cellar in the form of a knight holding a " dragier " [bonbonnière]. His gift to his sister Margaret, wife of Louis of Anjou, King of Sicily and Jerusalem, was a reliquary fashioned in a round shape, set with six rubies and six pearls all round the centre-piece; in the middle of one side was a cameo; in the middle of the other was a sapphire set in a white ground. The Duchess's gift to her sister-in-law was "a gold falcon enamelled in white, seated on a throne enamelled in green, garnished with a diamond, five rubies, and three pearl pendants." These gifts to Queen Margaret were the most costly of all the "Etrennes," the Duke's gift costing fifty ducats, that of his wife thirty-two.

Duke Louis's gift to his sister Maria, Duchess of Milan, the wife of Filippo Maria Visconti, was "an enamelled tree of gold, whereon was a man holding in his hand a monkey and three flying falcons"; a present that evidently was not easy of transport, as stress is laid on the fact that it was to be conveyed by "Monseigneur le mareschal de la Mouree a ma dame de Milan," doubtless from the difficulty that would be experienced in packing for shipment so awkward a decoration

as a monkey and three hawks on the wing,
even when they were imprisoned in settings
of gold and enamel.

The New Year's offerings that passed
between Louis and his Duchess were
as follows : " Paternostres de cassidonne
garnyes de vj pommes dargent dorees
propices a tenir pommes dambie " ; " vng
pendant d'or garny dune grosse perle dung
dymant, et dun rubys, et vng colier dor
garny de perles et de rubys ; lesquelles
Paternostres de cassideine et pendant des-
susdiz ma Damme donna destrenne a
Monseigneur et Monseigneur donna a
ma Damma ledit colier ledit jour de lan "
[Paternosters of chalcedony garnished
with six silver-gilt apples, designed to hold
amber *beads* (or grains of amber—if for
medicine) ; and a gold pendant adorned
with a great pearl, a diamond, and a ruby,
and a gold necklace adorned with pearls
and rubies ; which Paternosters of chalcedony and pendant above-mentioned my
Lady gave as a gift to my Lord, and my
Lord gave my Lady the said necklace on
the said New Year's Day].

The price of these gifts after the bargain had been made was twelve ducats for
the " Paternostres," and eighteen ducats
for the necklace. This was a moderate
sum in comparison with those generally
expended for this kind of presents.

Other gifts follow in great abundance
to the various members of the ducal
family, brothers, sisters, brothers-in-law,
sisters - in - law — all being remembered.
Though jewellery predominates to a great
extent, it does not exclude other things,
such as swords with elaborate sheaths;
table-knives, which were evidently a favourite form of present, and consisted of
one pair, sometimes even of two, costing
ten florins the pair, or twenty florins including the sheath; blades, gilt at Venice
and engraven with designs; caskets, in the
shape of apples, for amber (amber being a
drug much in vogue for its properties as
a perfume and as a medicine); and all
such kinds of gifts as might serve to knit
closer the bonds of family affection and
to brighten the New Year.

Nor were the members of the household

forgotten. The Duke presented eight
ladies of the Court each with a gold
chain; the price of these eight chains
amounted to a total of forty-six ducats.
To twelve other ladies were given rings;
each ring was formed of two stones, and
cost two ducats apiece; the stones were
either a ruby, a turquoise, or an emerald,
probably not of the first quality. Rings
were given freely, also purses, both by the
Duke and the Duchess. But nothing can
equal the quantity of caps presented by
the ducal couple, with which the list draws
to a close, and which figure under different names, assuming, at the same time,
different shapes, sizes, and colours. Some
are large, some are small; some have
strings, others have none; some are scarlet,
others are grey, while the fashion of a specially mentioned large red cap is one much
dwelt on, and evidently received much consideration at that epoch. The list of retainers who received these gifts is also
given, and must not be omitted here, consisting, as it does, of trumpeters, minstrels,
chambermen and chamberwomen, bakers,

butlers the literal rendering of the word *botelliers* or bottlers of the wine, caterers, cooks, scullerymen, poulterers, butchers, carriers, grooms, marshals, valets, messengers, upholsterers, gamekeepers, falconers, pastry-cooks, and other ordinary servants, equally of Monseigneur as of Madame, and of Messeigneurs the children. To all of these the Duke presented a New Year's gift of a florin apiece.

In almost every inventory some mention is made of the " Ring of St. Maurice," (the symbol which has already been spoken of as denoting the sovereign power and state in Savoy) and of "the true Cross." This latter, or more probably only a portion of it, was always kept in the Duke's room; though, during Duchess Yolande's life, the sacred relic was deposited in her apartment. An account is also given of this Duchess's dresses ; neither their number nor their fashion would commend themselves to the exigencies of to-day. We read first of "six manches de vellours cremesy brocard dor " [six sleeves of crimson velvet, brocaded with gold]. Then

comes "vne robe longue de Madame Yolant, quest de cremesi" [one long robe of
Madame Yolande of crimson]. It is remarkable how throughout these inventories the spelling is always changed, and
the same word is altered every time it occurs. Another gown, this one, however,
short, "de madicte Dame de cremesi"
[of my said Lady, of crimson], then another
one, also short, "de camelot de saye vio-
lete" [of violet silk camelot], and then
the list is complete. And a more modest
and limited wardrobe for so high and
puissant a dame could not well be found.
Considerable improvement as to quantity
and quality in the matter of wearing apparel is manifest in the inventory taken
after Duke Philibert's death in 1482, when
a step in advance had been made as to
luxury and elegance, for here we read of
fur-lined coats ; sable and marten are frequently used, though varied with the skins
of hares, of down, and of black Rouma-
nian lambs. All these articles, it would
seem, were given, after the Duke's demise,
to his valets and waiting-men.

It is easy to see from what has been
recorded in the foregoing pages that
wealth and extravagance went hand in
hand in the House of Savoy. But the day
of reckoning was not far off, and the successors of Amadeus VIII., who possessed
neither the intelligence nor the energy of
that prince, were forced to resort to every
kinds of means to make headway against
the financial difficulties that were steadily
accumulating, and to meet a legacy of
debt that each father passed on with the
same undeviating policy to his son and
successor. The primary cause of the
ever-increasing insolvency of "Casa Savoia" owed its origin undoubtedly to the
expeditions to the East and to Naples
of the " Conte Verde," and to the expenditure incurred by Amadeus VIII.,
when under the name of Felix V.
he assumed for a while the papal tiara.
The evil days were close at hand, and already Louis of Savoy, Amadeus's son and
successor, had to pawn much of his father's
goods to raise money and meet the demands constantly made on his purse,

either by the exigencies of the state or the wasteful expenditure of his wife, Anna of Cyprus.

On the occasion of the second marriage of his sister, Margaret of Savoy, with Louis, Duke of Bavaria, Louis pledged himself to give his sister a marriage portion of one hundred and twenty-five thousand florins "of the Rhine," twenty-five thousand of which were to be paid on the bride's arrival at Basle, and the rest within the space of the three following years. But the Duke of Savoy's finances were worse instead of better at the end of the allotted time, and in order to keep his word he sent a quantity of plate and jewels as security for the absent florins. These securities were to be deposited in a safe place in the town of Basle, and should the money not be forthcoming in the future, the plate and jewels were to remain confiscate to the Duke of Bavaria. Among a mass of silver-gilt cups, salvers, goblets, ewers, vases, jugs, and so forth, is mentioned also the tiara that Margaret's father had worn as Pope, which is described as "three

crowns of gold with many precious mar-
garites in the papal crown therein enclosed
and sealed." The state of the ducal exchequer must have fallen low to allow so
precious and interesting a relic to be sent
to a foreign country. Duke Lodovico
must either have felt very positive that
the day would come when this treasure
could be rescued, or else have had no
hope of better times and so permitted the
deluge of despair to swallow up all the associations of past, present, and future together. History has not revealed to us
whether the Duke's hopes or fears were
fulfilled.

Before closing the record of the personalties owned by the dukes and duchesses
of Savoy, the feasts and entertainments
given at the Court must not be omitted
from the consideration that they surely
deserve. Duchess Yolande was evidently
hospitably inclined, and the banquets given
under her auspices called forth on more
than one occasion the notice of the Court-
chroniclers. Those that elicit the most
comment were given to the ambassadors

of the Dukes of Milan and of Burgundy in the year 1474, and to the Prince of Taranto, the son of the King of Sicily, in January of the following year. But these pale before the glories of the festival that took place in December, 1476, when the guests were Yolande's own son and his wife, the Count and Countess of Geneva.

The "bill of expenses" is drawn up by one Lancelot de Lans, whose profession was that of "gentleman of the mouth" (gentiluomo di bocca), implying doubtless that all questions as to food and supplies for the mouth were under his care and supervision. A difficult and thankless post to fill, if tastes were as fastidious and exacting as they are nowadays! The expenses refer to the entertainment and presents provided for the guests, to the utter exclusion (at least here) of the dishes and viands set upon the board. The first articles to be provided are pewter covers wherewith to protect what are here spoken of as "entremes"; by this word is meant "all that occurred between the courses," and, in the Middle Ages, the diversion which took place during an interval of the repast. Under these covers were dresses, described as "liveries," streaked with gold and silver, and which were destined as gifts for the guests. Then followed heads of pigs and of boars, invariably gilded and bedecked with trimmings and devices. After these came the triumphal car, or "baldacchino" (a device of no small account in the feast), on which were placed a Captain and four damsels, all armed with gold and silver weapons, with banners and standards waving about them; the maidens were adorned with locks of artificial hair, whereof the tresses, several yards in length, fell curling to the ground, or floated in the breeze as the chariot moved along on its triumphal way.

There were minstrels; there were dancers, mummers, and masqueraders; and above all there was a giant effigy called "Goliath," whose make-up must have caused considerable trouble, to say nothing of the expense. For first of all there was the potter's clay for the mould wherein he was to be cast, together with all the

consequent items for that process; then
came the arms for making "Goliath" a
complete man of war,—his banners, his
lances, and his daggers, and finally his
"large head." However, when all was
told, the price for so satisfactory a produc-
tion was not more than one florin; though
this did not include the hair for "Goliath,"
which has a separate notice all to itself,
being composed of old sheep's wool (the
fact of the wool being old is dwelt on,
though the merits as to its antiquity are
not revealed), and costing "vj gros." The
sempstresses' bill came to thirteen florins.
In this was comprised the labour for making and sewing on the fringes that went
not only round the knights' banners, but
also about the dishes, the stitching needed
by the men-at-arms, and the supplying of
the hair for the maidens on the car, for
each of whom no less than four yards
of tresses were required. A numerous
list is given of the other odds and ends
needed for the occasion, such as candles,
string, cord, hooks, cloth, wax-flowers in
the shape of fleurs-de-lys, copper-wire for

making crowns, lanterns, ostrich feathers for the masqueraders, and two for the Duchess, dresses for the mummers and the minstrels, jerkins, gilt and silvered leather for the linings of caps and edging of waistcoats and "justacorps," silk, fustian, and other materials, together with the money paid to the carpenters, sempstresses, gilders, painters, furriers, etc. These make up a sum total of over two hundred and fifteen florins.

ARMS OF HUMBERT OF THE WHITE HANDS.

Amedeus IX

Ludovici filius, Sabaudie Dux III a Carolo. XXI natus Thauris die prima Februarÿ Ann. 1435. Manu et corpore imbecillus, temperatus et ÷, equus et superanty fuisse in minimis incommodis temperatus. Æmecus, qui plurimū fuis sunt authentique. A ÷ P. Pontifice. commis et interpones appui us intam multa in suum ÷ pares expositione commit singulus rebus, que a ÷ demus. Pulcrorumque utilitatem censere ÷ sumut. Sic utham incus, sanctequo anumam, Vercellis, idio charis inter Amici karitus Satur. Anno 1472, sepultusque in Sant ÷ fine, ur unus idio charis inter Amici karitus Satur.

CHAPTER III

THE Salic law was in full force in Savoy. The opposition with which it
had been combated by the daughters of
the House of Savoy had been vehement
and determined ; but their resistance had
been in vain, and no princess of the dynasty could sit on the throne of her forefathers, or transmit her rights to that
throne to any of her heirs. But, as if to
atone for this restriction, a destiny stronger
than any law, in a spirit of contradiction

(so often to be found where arrogant forces have asserted themselves), had brought compensation in a shape altogether unlooked for, and in a manner that was certainly never demanded. In no other European history are the same number of minorities to be met as in that of the House of Savoy. Invariably these minorities were watched over and directed by princesses who had made Savoy the land of their adoption, and who by their devotion might well claim from it the same love and respect which has ever been conceded to the direct descendants of Humbert of the White Hands. These minorities, with a few exceptions, may be dated from the reign of Amadeus IX. and his wife, Yolande of France, when, to quote a modern writer, "The reign of Amadeus IX. inaugurated that long series of regencies, which, although entrusted to women of masculine qualities, brought the state of Savoy, all the same, to the very verge of absolute ruin."[1]

[1] Bertolotti, Davide, *Istoria della R. Casa di Savoia*, p. 107, Milano, 1830.

The pair were affianced when still in the
cradle, the bride-elect being but two years
old, and her plighted bridegroom a year
younger. The contract for the marriage
was drawn up at Tours (where Yolande
was born the 6th of August, 1434) by her
father, Charles VII., and the ambassadors
of Amadeus VIII., the bridegroom's grandfather. In conformity with a rule in vogue
in Savoy, the child was sent soon after
to be educated in the country of her
adoption, from her earliest youth to learn
the language, customs, and traditions of
the land which henceforth she was to consider her own.

The period when Yolande first arrived
in Savoy was one of prosperity for the
country. Amadeus VIII. had brought
the duchy to a flourishing condition ; and
the decay that set in during the reign of
his son Louis was too gradual to be as
yet felt. "The Sabaudian state began to
decline, owing to the maladministration of
the new Duke [Louis], flighty, a lover
of display, effeminate, and unable to move
a step without his wife, the beautiful Anna

of Cyprus, who filled his Court with Cypriots, to the annoyance and envy of the nobles of Savoy." [1]

What share Yolande took in the brilliant, luxurious, and frivolous Court no record relates.   Her first actual appearance in public was evidently in 1451, when, at the age of seventeen, she was present at the marriage of her brother Louis, Dauphin of France, with Charlotte of Savoy, eldest daughter of Duke Louis and Anna of Cyprus.   This marriage, though opposed by King Charles VII., was promoted by the bride's parents, who were proud of the alliance, and who hoped by it to secure the future king of France as an unalterable ally to the cause and interests of Savoy.   Charles VII. had endeavoured in vain to prevent the marriage ; he was angry at the manner in which his heir had been "caught"; and he resolved to march against Duke Louis to punish him for his share in a transaction which annoyed him doubly, as monarch and as father.

[1] Dina, Achille, *Yolanda, Duchessa di Savoia e la Ribellione Sabauda nel* 1471, p. 6.   Alba, 1892.

The intervention of the Papal Legate was invoked to allay the King's wrath, but a more timely intervention arose at that moment in an invasion of the English into France. Charles was only too glad to conclude peace with his kinsman of Savoy and to devote himself to the more troublesome neighbour. This peace was ratified by the marriage of the Prince of Piedmont and Yolande of France, which took place in 1452, the bride having attained the age of eighteen, and the bridegroom being only seventeen. The young couple divided the earlier part of their married life between the provinces of Vaud and Bresse; they were not on the best of terms with the reigning Duke and Duchess, and preferred to pass their days far from a Court whose frivolity excited their disdain, and whose reckless display and extravagance they were unable to restrain.

It was an anxious time for Savoy, and not over quiet for France, Burgundy, or Milan. In Milan the line of the Visconti had just become extinct, and the Duke of Savoy, neglecting the golden opportunity

to subjugate the Milanese and thus to
lay the basis of a powerful state in
Italy, allowed himself to be outwitted by
his far cleverer and more energetic rival,
Francesco Sforza, who fixed himself and
his dynasty on the throne of Milan to the
utter exclusion of the House of Savoy.

By the death of King Charles VII., in
1461, the Dauphin Louis became King of
France. Savoy, after having made but a
feeble effort to shake off the encroaching
policy of Charles, weak though that policy
had been, was absolutely unable to assert
herself against the wiles, the ingenuity,
and the unscrupulousness of Louis XI.
In Burgundy, the turbulent, warlike Count
of Charalois, soon to succeed his father as
Duke Charles the Bold, was adding to the
condition of unrest of all around him, by
his alliances first with one power, then
with another, and by the necessity which
obliged him to keep always on the alert
against the treachery, ability, and cunning
of his traitorous cousin and so-called friend,
the King of France.

Amid the universal turbulence engen-

dered by the rule of such men, Savoy could
not hope for a quiet existence ; and the
fever of agitation spread its contagion into
the very heart of the country, bringing
misery, civil war, and desolation. Of all
the restless spirits running on the earth—
and at that moment their name was legion
—the most restless perhaps was Philip of
Savoy, Count of Bresse, fifth son of Louis
and Anna, generally known by the nickname he had adopted for himself of " Lack-
land " (Sans Terre) in ironic allusion to
the small patrimony bestowed on him by
his father. This prince, whose intriguing
nature had disordered his father's reign,
and hastened, it is said, his mother's end,
was not minded to accept without a struggle the position into which affairs were
drifting in Savoy. His brother, Amadeus
IX., whose health was undermined by epi-
lepsy and whose thoughts were wholly absorbed by heavenly things, had wished,
when his father's death called him to the
throne in 1465, to renounce that dignity
and devote himself exclusively to a life of
seclusion and contemplation. But his

wife, Yolande, resolutely opposed his
intentions, and, for the sake of her children, persuaded her husband to remain at
the head of affairs, which she undertook to
administer in his name, in order to oust
her ambitious brother-in-law and to maintain the right of succession for her sons.
The Venetian Orator, Dandolo, reporting
from Savoy at this moment to his government, writes : " I signify to you how the
ill-health of the Duke is known to all,
while his memory fails him and his answers
are given at random ; Madama [Yolande]
governs, and she certainly attends to her
words and doings ; if it is lawful to form a
judgment in forty-three days, she seemed
to me humane, a sagacious lady, and
filled with the dignity due to her position ;
but she is only a woman." The disdain
expressed in the Orator's concluding words,
" ma ĕ pur donna," is the more noticeable
as circumstances were to emphasise its
truth, and to stamp upon Yolande's regency
the brand of misfortune for Savoy, and the
need through succeeding years for the
firm hand and the powerful rule of a man.

In order to maintain the rights claimed by her for her children, Yolande had to keep a sharp lookout on three sides from which danger threatened. On one side was her brother, Louis XI., the more to be feared since, under the mask of acting as her protector and adviser, he veiled the deepest designs on the state entrusted to her care ; on another side was Charles the Bold, Duke of Burgundy, whose enmity with Louis induced all who were hostile to that monarch to throw in their lot with the Duke and to swell the ranks of Burgundy into a formidable and numerous host ; and lastly, there were her brothers-in-law, Philip, Count of Bresse, James, Count of Romont, and John Louis, Bishop of Geneva.

In France, the League for the Public Good had just been formed against King Louis by his most powerful vassals and subjects ; the Dukes of Bourbon and Burgundy had joined it ; and Amadeus of Savoy was urged on one hand by the Leaguers to espouse their cause, while on the other King Louis claimed his assistance and support. In conformity with the wishes and injunctions of his wife, Amadeus gave adherence to the French monarch, a measure which at once prompted his brothers to espouse the cause of the League. The annoyance of these princes was heightened when, soon afterwards, Yolande, chiefly through the instrumentality of Louis XI., was named Regent of the duchy, her husband, though he did not abdicate, desiring his subjects to obey her in all things. This nomination, approved by the Three States, by the nobles, and by the people of Savoy, gave still further offence to the Duke's brothers, especially to Count Philip. The constant efforts made by the Count to possess himself of the regency, his plots for deposing Yolande, her counter-plots to defeat his aims, led to a series of alliances, negotiations, diplomatic missions, and secret understandings, wherein each party tried to circumvent and outdo the other. These intrigues were joined in by the King of France, by Duke Charles of Burgundy, and by Duke Galeazzo Maria

Sforza, and involved the different actors
in a succession of frauds, double-dealings,
and subtleties so complex and intricate
that they are very difficult to unravel.

Count Philip's first movement against
Yolande was in 1471, when, seeing how
absolutely he was debarred from share in
the government, he determined to possess
himself of the persons of the Duke and
Duchess, and then to appoint himself
ruler.   Some hint of his intentions reached
the Duchess.   She at once repaired with
her husband and children to Montmélian,
which was better fortified than Chambéry,
where the Court had been till then.   There
Philip besieged them.   One of the gates
of the town having been gained by treachery, Philip entered Montmélian.   At his
approach, the ducal party took refuge in
the citadel, and after eight days' parleying,
the Regent, who looked in vain for help
from France, had to surrender to her
brother-in-law.

Amadeus was at once conveyed to
Chambéry, but Yolande (who on occasions showed herself to be her brother's

own sister!), was seized with an unexpected illness and professed to be unable
to start with her husband, whom she would
follow, she said, the next day.   Philip accordingly set out with Amadeus, while the
Counts of Romont and of Geneva stayed
behind with Yolande, her children, and
her ladies-in-waiting.   It was then ar-
ranged that they should dine at Apremont
the next day, and sup at Chambéry.   The
first part of this plan was carried out ; but
after dinner, when all was in readiness to
start for Chambéry, the Duchess suddenly
declared she could go no further then, but
that she would overtake them the day following ; and to keep up the deceit she sent
forward all the kitchen apparatus, together
with the master of her household.   That
evening the Count of Geneva took leave
of her, confidently expecting to see her
again next morning.   But hardly was she
alone than she despatched advices to her
faithful servitors, the Seigneurs of Com-
minges and Miolans, to come at midnight
to her rescue, and, at a signal of lighted
fires, to approach the castle walls.   After

supper, she dismissed her male attendants, enjoining on them to go and sleep, as they would have to rise early next morning ; then, having carefully bolted the doors, she, her children, and her ladies made ready for their departure. At the appointed hour the signals were given ; part of the armed men under the Count of Miolans drew near to the castle, and Yolande, who had secreted the keys, opened a postern gate through which she and her party slipped out and mounted on horseback, while Miolans posted his followers in the castle.

The Duchess rode to La Bussière, and passed the rest of the night in a monastery, the following morning going on to Grenoble, where she was received with great honours.   Meanwhile, Count Philip had reached Chambéry, and having in his power the person of the reigning Duke, he resolved to derive from this circumstance all the advantages otherwise denied him.   He convoked the Three States in Amadeus's name, and together with his brother, the Count of Romont, proceeded to institute a form of government. Yolande, far from being overawed at the boldness of these measures, uttered her protest : she at once announced that the government of the land depended solely on herself, and she wrote imperious letters to the governors of all of the fortresses throughout the duchy, forbidding them, under penalty of death and forfeiture of their goods, to deliver up their castles to anyone, whoever he might be, without an express order from her or from her " fair son, the Prince Charles," whose arrival from France she was then looking for with the greatest eagerness. She sent messengers to the Three States to thank them for their expressions of devotion and fidelity; help was also demanded from Milan ; and Hugues de Montfaucon was despatched to France to entreat the King not to delay in hastening her son's arrival.

For the moment the hopes of peace and deliverance were centred round the person of the Prince of Piedmont, whose residence in France at his uncle's Court was intended to give him an education and an

experience that would stand him in good
stead in after years. The hopes of the
presence of the Heir-apparent among his
own subjects, and of the loyalty to be
evoked by the thought of his advent, as
well as the joy that Yolande felt over her
son's arrival, when his sympathy, counsel,
and support would enable her to make
a still firmer front against the assaults of
her brothers-in-law, were all doomed to a
cruel disappointment. The Prince, only
sixteen years old, put himself at the head
of eight thousand archers (the nucleus of
that famous body of light infantry, the first
example of a standing army, which, instituted in 1448 by Charles VII., had been in-
creased three years previously to no less
than fifty thousand men by Louis XI.), and
set off to the rescue of his parents. But at
Orleans he was struck down by a fatal at-
tack of pneumonia, and on the morning
of the 12th of July, 1471, the news of his
death reached poor Yolande. The shock
might well have broken her heart and
crushed her spirit and courage: Heaven
itself seemed to have forsaken her for the

time, and she must have needed all her faith, and all the vigour and energy of her mind to face such a blow.

The appeals, however, to her powerful neighbours had not been in vain ; and, among others, the Duke of Milan sent his ambassador, one Antonio d'Appiano, to report on the condition of affairs in Savoy, and to see to what extent his help would be required. Appiano was also requested to inform Galeazzo about Yolande's children, which he accordingly did in the following terms : "This My Lady has three male children : the eldest about five years, intelligent, thin, and always of a bad colour because he has the malady of the stone, and this was told me by His Majesty himself . . . and since the death of the other prince he is called Monsignore and Prince and Heir, seeing that the duchy will devolve on him. The second is about two and a half to three years, and is a lively boy of a somewhat serious countenance and of a good colour; four days ago he was a little indisposed. The third is but one year old, lively, but a bit serious in his aspect. She has two daughters, the eldest of about eight years old, and the second from six to seven to my thinking. Both have but little colour; but are decidedly nice-looking and capable of being present at table and at vespers, where they always read the office ; and at table with My Lady they have very good manners ; likewise, the two eldest boys are always at table, where all are served in a proper manner by their respective serving-women." [1]

Duchess Yolande also suffered from that painful "malady of the stone," and when to this were added the anxieties as to her husband's health, the cares of state, the vigilance that had always to be maintained against the open and secret animosity of her brothers-in-law, it needs no great stretch of the imagination to realise the weight and burden under which she had to live. Her political embarrassments were removed for a while by the help sent to her from France and Milan ; and Count

[1] *Lettera di Antonio d' Appiano*, Chambéry, 9 Settembre. 1471.

Philip, seeing that his best policy was to
cease for the present from his unnatural
persecution, consented to an agreement
with his sister-in-law, whose position as
Regent he now promised to recognise,
while she was to consent to the formation
of a Council in which the Princes of Savoy
were also to have a voice. After the
signing of this treaty, Amadeus was set
free, and the husband and wife met again
at Chambéry—the Duke in a precarious
state of health engendered by the loss of
his eldest son, and the Duchess worn by
all she had gone through, and terrified,
too, by the misery which she foresaw only
too clearly awaited her from the Duke's
altered condition. The pair removed at
once to Vercelli, where it was hoped that
change of air and scene would restore
Amadeus's health and reinvigorate the
Duchess, whose condition required rest
and freedom from anxiety.

The Court had hardly been settled five
months at Vercelli when the Duke became
alarmingly ill. The Duchess, whose love
and concern revealed at once to her the

gravity of the case, applied to the Duke of Milan in her need, and begged him to send instantly one of his most skilful physicians. Two of his most learned and trusted doctors came to Vercelli; but their skill was in vain, and Amadeus expired on the 30th of March, 1472, aged only thirty-seven years, his last words being: "Do justice and judgment, and love the poor, and God will give you peace at the last." The piety and goodness of Amadeus IX. gained for him intense veneration during his life; the patience with which he bore a trial heavy enough to depress the bravest spirit cannot be sufficiently admired, for against this trial it is said he never was heard to utter one word of complaint, nor ever to murmur at the heavy cross laid on him. His marvellous care for the poor was the characteristic of his life, and it is related of him that on one occasion when the Duke of Milan, who had come to visit him, inquired where he kept his hounds, he answered, pointing to a group of poor people: "There you see them, and with that pack I trust to se-

cure to myself a glorious prey and obtain
through them the joys of Paradise." In
his latter years, he denied himself in every
way he could, selling even his jewels, including, it is said, the insignia of the
Order of the Collar, and all that he possessed of luxury and grandeur, to give to
the poor, often parting even with much of
his wardrobe. His memory was held in
such veneration that he was enrolled in the
number of the Saints, and a decree of
Innocent XI. set apart the 30th of March
as the day dedicated henceforward to the
" Blessed Amadeus of Savoy."

The Prince of Piedmont being only
seven years old at the time of his father's
death, his mother Yolande was appointed
Regent and guardian by the unanimous
voice of the Three States and by popular
acclamation ; and she lost no time in de-
spatching a messenger to her brother,
King Louis, to inform him of her husband's death, and to implore his protection
for herself, her children, and the state
committed to her trust. But Duchess
Yolande did not confine herself to appeals

AMADEUS IX.

for earthly aid ; two beautiful prayers
composed by her at this period have come
down to us, and show by their touching
tone of entreaty and humility the earnest-
ness of her petition.   The first of these
prayers is :

"Feit a la doulce Mere de Dieu per
grant ferueur et deuocion pour ly donner
et oufrir elle et ses enfans et tout son fait.

JHESUS MARIA

Glorieuse vierge Marie, mere de Dieu
et madame ma maistresse, je Yolant de
France, miserable pecheresse et vostre esclaue, confesse et vous promet de toute sa
puissance, per la foy quelle doit a Dieu et
a Vous, et confesse vous auoir fait hommage de corps et de ame et de biens, et
de rechief vous donne son corps et same,
et vous baille toutes la signorie et ses enfans et le pais, et toutes la justice et puissance quelle at en ce monde, a votre
gouuernement, et sen demetz et le vous
remetz, et de ceste heure en avant vous
rent son corps et son ame et ses enfans,
prais et signoire, et Vous supplie que laye
pour recommandes et les veulliez garder

de leurs ennemys et de tout ce qui leur
porroit nuyre, et aussy me veullie garder a lheure de la mort de lennemy et
de sa puissance, car je il renunce, et au
monde aussy.   Et se ma personne per
fragillite tonboit en peche, que a lheure
de la mort ilz ne me puisse riens demander, car je tay fait toute ma vie
depuis ma cognoissance hommaige, et
suis tesclaue.   Et en tesmoing du dit
homage jeu dit tous les jours XV Aue
Maria.   Et en tesmoing de verite, et
aussy que tout ce que yai escript de ma
main je veult qui soit fait.   Et depuis ma
naissance jusques a la fin lennemy ne me
puisse riens demander en corps ne ame, et
aussy le pais, lequelz je vous donne.   Jay
escript ces presentes de ma main et sellez
de mon seel a Pinerol le xij jours de
septembre.

"Vostre miserable esclaue,

"YOLANT DE FRANCE.

Monseigneur sainct Francois et vous
Marie Magdelaine, je vous supplie, presentes ceste lectre a la vierge Marie, et a
lheure de la mort soiez en mes tesmoing

contre lennemy et protestes a mon bon
ange comme a mes aduocat que je ne suis
que a la virge Marie."

[Made to the sweet Mother of God
through great fervour and devotion, to
give her and offer to her herself, her children and all that she does.

JESUS MARIA

Glorious Virgin Mary, Mother of God
and my Lady Mistress, I, Yolande of
France, miserable sinner and your slave,
confess and promise you with all my
might, by the faith which I owe to God
and to you, and confess to have paid you
homage with body and soul and goods,
and hereby give you my body and soul,
and witness to you all my signory, my
children and the country, and all the justice and power which I have in this world,
to your government, and put it away
from myself, and put it in your hands,
and at this hour render to you, in advance,
my body, and soul, and my children, country, and signory, and beg your intercession
for them, and that you will guard them
from their enemies and from all that might

injure them, and also that you will guard
me at the hour of my death from the
enemy and from his power, for I renounce
him and the world also. And if I
should through frailty fall into sin, that
at the hour of my death he may have no
power over me, for all my life since I was
conscious, I have paid thee homage and
am thy slave, and in witness of the said
homage I have said, every day, fifteen
Ave Marias. And in witness of the truth
I will that all I have written with my hand
should be done. And from my birth even
to the end let the enemy ask nothing of
me in body or soul—or of the country
which I give to you. I have written this
present with my hand, and seal it with
my seal at Pinerol the twelfth day of
September.

Your miserable slave,

YOLANDE DE FRANCE.

My Lord St. Francis, and you, Mary
Magdalen, I pray you, present this letter
to the Virgin Mary, and at the hour of
my death be my witnesses against the
enemy, and declare to my good angel as

well as to my advocate that I belong only
to the Virgin Mary.]

Another prayer again to the Blessed
Virgin from her "miserable slave, Yolant de France," as she so touchingly
calls herself, runs as follows :

" JHESUS MARIA

A vous, glorieuse virge Marie, mere de
Dieu et madame et maistresse, je Yolant
de France, pouure pecheresse et vostre
talliable et esclaue, tant comme amini-
streresse et tutri de la Duchie de Sauoye
et de Piémon et aultres signorie aproue
et ratifie la lectre escripte cy deuant. Et
premierement en ly donant mon dit corps
et ame et mes enfans, et ly remetz toutes
la puissance que per les Estas ma estee
donnee, Vous supplia que il vous plaise la
accepter, et gouuerner le dit pais et enfans
et moy aussy et les garder de leurs ennemys, en maniere que puisse faire chose
quapres ceste mortelle vye puisse auoir la
pardurable. Et de ceste heure me demetz de toute ma puissance et la vous
remetz. Et, que chose que per fragillite
face ou puisse ferez contre vostre volente,

proteste que a lheure de la mort ne me puisse riens demander lennemy, car je renunces a luy et a tous ses fais et au monde aussy. Et pour hommage vous dit tous les jours de ma vye XV Aue Maria cy en signe destre vostre tallable. Vous supplians, glorieuse Mere de Dieu, que a lheure de ma mort en veulliez estre mon tesmoing, et que je ne veult ne entent qui puisse auoir puissance sur moy, et veult viure et morir en ta loy et comme bonne crestienne. Et en tesmoing de verite ay conforme et approuue la premiere lectre estre vaillable, et ceste cy, toutes escriptes de ma main et selee de ma tutee et administracion.

" Vostre tres humble et miserable esclaue
            "YOLANT DE FRANCE.

Monseigneur sainct Francois, et vous Marie Magdelayne presente ceste lectre a la glorieuse vierge Marie, protestant aucques sainct Jaques, a qui je suis pelerine, que je ne suis que a elle, et elle me veulle recepuoir mon corps et tout mes enfans et pais en ceste mortelle vye, et lame quant elle partira de ce poures corps,

affin que ses dit soient veritable quelle est
aduocate des pecheurs, desquelx je me
tien, voire des plus poures, et jen demande
mon bon Angel en tesmoing."

[JESUS MARIA

To you, glorious Virgin Mary, Mother
of God, and my lady and mistress, I Yolande of France, poor sinner and your
bondwoman and slave, as well as admin-
istratrix and *tutrix* of the Duchy of Savoy
and of Piedmont and of other signories,
approve and ratify the letter written
herewith. And first in giving you my
said body and soul and my children and
putting into your hands all the power
which the States have given me, I sup-
plicate you that it may please you to
accept them, and to govern the said
country and children and me also, and
to guard them from their enemies in
order that they may do such things that
after this mortal life they may have life
everlasting. And from this hour, I put
away all my power, and put it in your
hands. And whatever through frailty I
have done or may do against your will

let the enemy at the hour of my death
demand nothing of me, for I renounce
him and all his works and the world
also.   And for homage I have said to
you all the days of my life fifteen Ave
Marias, in sign that I am your bondwoman.   Supplicating you, glorious Mother
of God, that at the hour of my death you
will be my witness, and that I neither
wish nor intend that *he* should have
any power over me, and I wish to live
and die in your law and as a good Christian.   And in witness of the truth, I con-
firm and approve the first letter to be
valid, and this also, all written with my
hand and sealed, of my tutorship and administration.

Your very humble and miserable slave,
YOLANDE DE FRANCE.

My Lord St. Francis, and you Mary
Magdalen, present this letter to the
glorious Virgin Mary, declaring as well
as St. James, whose pilgrim I am, that
I am hers only, and that she will receive my body and all my children and
country in this mortal life, and my soul

when it shall depart from this poor body,
on to the end in order that her words may
be true that she is the advocate of sinners,
of whom I am one, and one of the poor-
est and I call my good angel to witness
this.]

These two "letters" (as Duchess Yolande herself calls them) are followed by
an official note which establishes their au-
thenticity, and which then goes on to say :
"The valiant Lady had given these letters to one of her women, forbidding her
to shew them to anyone, and enjoining on
her that when she saw the hour of her
death to be drawing nigh, to bring them
and place them between her hands.   But
this woman was so taken aback by this
death that she forgot the command of her
Lady and mistress, and when she perceived her omission she then brought
them.   The said letters were so highly
valued by the gentlemen of the Council
that her noble daughter, our reverend
Lady and mother, Sister Louise of Savoy,
was powerless to obtain these letters written in the handwriting of her Lady-mother

for her own, for it was willed that they should remain in the House of Savoy. Therefore, her said noble daughter copied them and kept them ever by her, carrying them always religiously about with her things which she loved right dearly."

In the meanwhile the petition made by the widowed Duchess to Louis XI. for help—unluckily for Savoy—was responded to in the manner habitual to that monarch. He had been long anxious to establish a hold upon Savoy, and Yolande's appeal gave him the opportunity he wanted without even entailing on him the usual amount of lying, deceiving, and cheating which he generally practised before conferring on his petitioner his so-called "help." The treachery with which he supported Philip of Bresse, and incited him to rebel against the Regent while avowedly espousing her cause was the more contemptible in one who was her brother, and posed as the guardian of her children and herself.

The wiles employed by Louis XI. and Count Philip were deceitful in the extreme, but Yolande was far too wary to be deceived. The answer that she returned to Philip when, soon after her husband's death, the Count suggested that a visit from his wife might cheer her, showed that she was alive to his attempts to force his way into her Court and thence to obtain a footing in her Council. Philip had said that his wife was not only willing to pay a visit, but also to live with the Duchess. Yolande's reply was: This is not the time in which she should come; she, Madame, being on this occasion sad and tearful, while she (Count Philip's wife) was a bride; that brides desired to be entertained in a fit manner, and that for the moment no entertainments could be looked for from her.[1]

In the month of September following Amadeus's death Yolande gave birth to a posthumous son, and she asked the Duke of Milan to act as godfather, and to hold the child at the font. The Duke begged to be excused from the latter function, pleading that he was ill adapted for such

[1] *Lettera del Vescovo di Como*, Vercelli, 18 Aprile, 1472.

solemnities and ceremonies (di essere mal
apto ad simile solemnitate et ceremonie).
The Duchess on being told of this excuse
by the Duke's Orator answered, laughing,
"that the Duke would not have to do
other than place his hand upon him, for
though it is true and customary that the
first godfather should hold the infant in
his arms at the baptism . . . such a
charge could not be laid on great seigneurs."[1]   The Duke of Bari, afterwards so
famous as Lodovico the Moor, Duke of
Milan, acted in his brother's stead; and
the infant, who only lived a few months,
received the names of Claud Galeazzo.

The bonds of kinship existing between
the House of Savoy and the Sforza family were still further strengthened by the
betrothal of the young Duke Philibert of
Savoy with Bianca Maria, daughter of
Galeazzo and Bona of Savoy; but of the
dependence to be placed on Milan as an
ally Duchess Yolande must have felt somewhat uncertain if the following incident is

[1] *Lettera di Antonio d'Appiano*, Vercelli, 21 Settembre,
1472.

to be taken as an example of Duke Galeazzo's trustworthiness. The Duke had declared that he desired to be always allied to Savoy, and that "neither a King of France or God Himself, were He to come down to earth, should cause him to change his mind"; but on Yolande's applying to him for a body of men to assist in the defence of Montmélian and Chambéry, he declined to send them, the excuse being that his infantry were not used to such places, and that she had better apply to the Duke of Burgundy for help on the other side of the Alps. Truly a reliable friend and neighbour, this Lord of Milan, and one in whom a persecuted, defenceless woman might well feel confidence in the hour of need !

And indeed, Duchess Yolande must often have been at her wits' end to know to whom to apply in her distress. Her brother, the King of France, though professedly fond of her, thought more of getting the Duchy of Savoy into his clutches than of protecting its Duchess, and pursued his policy of fraud, cunning,

and hypocrisy, regardless of his sister.
Her brother-in-law, Count Philip of
Bresse, was her implacable foe, who played
into the hands of Louis XI. with a view
to further his own ends, oblivious alike
of patriotism or of family feeling.   The
Duke of Milan was dominated by a policy
as unstable as it was selfish ; and the Regent, in her despair, turned at last to
Charles the Bold, Duke of Burgundy, as
an ally on whom she might place some
trust, and whose own interest might induce him to be faithful.

The Duke, on his side, was anxious to
secure the Duchess to his interests.   His
overthrow by the Swiss at Grandson (1476)
had greatly diminished his prestige, besides seriously damaging his financial condition ; it had also given him a shock as
to the position in which his allies would
regard him, and he felt it necessary to
grapple more closely than ever to his
cause those whom he could still consider
his friends.   He invited the Duchess to
meet him at Lausanne to confer with him
as to the state of affairs, and several inter-

VIEW OF MONCALIERI, WHERE YOLANDE OF FRANCE DIED.

views took place between them, to the rage
and annoyance of Louis XI., who in after
times taunted his sister with the negotiations with his enemy, and resented bit-
terly her conduct in acting for the welfare
of Savoy rather than for the advantage of
France. The defeat of Charles of Burgundy on the battle-field of Morat, where
a troop of men and officers sent by Yolande to the assistance of the Duke were
all killed, served still further to blast his
reputation ; and Yolande, fearing that she
had thrown in her lot with the losing side,
began to consider the wisdom of abandon-
ing Charles, and of ingratiating herself
anew with Louis.

This phase of Duchess Yolande's character is not a pleasant one to dwell on,
but though her tactics cannot be excused,
they may be condoned to some extent
when one reflects on the strategies of
the day (perhaps, too, of all days when
politics and self-interest come in !), and
remembers that probably some of her
brother's tendencies ran in her veins also.
Her readiness to forsake Duke Charles

and to make up to King Louis excited
the indignation of the Burgundian Duke,
but he determined to dissemble his wrath
and to pretend to believe in her all the
same.

This feint, however, he did not long continue ; he considered that it would be
more to his advantage to secure possession of the Duchess and of her son, and
he lost no time in putting his resolve
into execution. The Duchess was at that
moment at Geneva, intending to return
to Piedmont, and had had an interview
with Charles, when he had tried to persuade her to retire to his states, where
she would be safer than in Switzerland or
in her own domains.   Yolande refused to
comply with the Duke's suggestions, and
the Duke then commissioned his chamberlain, Olivier de la Marche, to carry off the
Duchess and Duke Philibert without further discussion. This order was altogether
unacceptable to Olivier ; "I did what he
ordered me, against my heart," he says,
"because the Duke, my master, was such
that he willed that one did what he com-

manded on pain of losing one's head."[1]
The interview between Duke Charles and
Duchess Yolande had taken place at a
spot called St. Cloud, two miles outside
Geneva, and after the Duke had cere-
moniously taken leave of Yolande she
started with an escort of cavalry to return
to Geneva.

It was nightfall ; the Duchess was in
her litter, her children riding beside her,
when, on a sudden, a company of horse-
men rushed on the party, and Olivier de
la Marche, with a following of six hundred
horse, pounced down on the ducal cortège.
Fighting began at once, swords flashed,
blood flowed, blows were freely given and
exchanged, and in the scuffle the Duchess's
litter was overturned.   She herself, her
second son Charles, and her daughters
Marie and Louise were taken prisoners,
but owing to the devotion and valour of
the Lords of Racconigi, of Riparolo, and of
La Villette, the little Duke Philibert and
his brother James Louis were saved from
the clutches of Charles the Bold, and car-

[1] See Appendix.

ried off safely to Chambéry, from whence they were afterwards removed to the Court of their uncle of France for greater safety. The Duke of Burgundy received the company very grumpily, and was much put out at the escape of Duke Philibert, and Olivier says that his life was in danger, owing to his having failed in seizing the person of the young Duke. Charles's ill-humour was so great he refused to see the Duchess; and having tried in vain through one of his councillors to induce Yolande to send for her eldest son, he ordered the prisoners to be removed, first to the Castle of Rochefort and then to Rouvre.

The Duchess's Court at Geneva made incessant moanings, weepings, and lamentations over their mistress's captivity, " and who had heard and seen their tears and sighs would certainly have felt great compassion and pity; and I know not if the laments of the Magdalen were as piteous with which she washed the feet of the Redeemer with tears. And Duke Philibert, your son, said: ' Weep no more, I pray

you. God will give me grace, and with the
help of our relations and good friends we
will be avenged.'"[1] Savoy was indeed for
the moment in a pitiable plight : the Regent, with one of her sons and two of her
daughters, was a prisoner in the hands of
a prince who till then had been considered
a friend; the Duke, one of his brothers,
and the chief places of the land were in
the power of the King of France; the
state was governed by two princes whose
only thought and aim was personal ambition and private vengeance. Such a condition of things was one not easily to be
remedied.

The sensation produced by the Duchess's captivity showed itself in different
ways : Louis XI. determined to turn it
to account in procuring for himself that
hold over the affairs of Savoy against
which his sister had always maintained
a firm resistance; the princes of Savoy
judged the opportunity an excellent one
for making good their pretensions to the

[1] *Lettera di Antonio d'Appiano al Duca di Milano*, Ginevra,
29 Giúgno, 1476, V. Gingins. Dep. cccxxv.

government of the country; while the country itself deplored the absence of a Regent whose rule had inspired confidence, wielded as everyone knew it to be for the real welfare and advancement of Savoy.

SEAL OF THOMAS I., COUNT OF SAVOY.

Yolande's courage was undaunted. She was not guarded rigorously enough to be prevented from corresponding with her friends, and she lost no time in communicating with them as to the means to be employed for effecting her release. She despatched her secretary, one Cavoretto, to her brother, King Louis, entrusting him with a ring which his Majesty had given her on her wedding-day, and imploring the King by this sign to procure her freedom. But such a move was far from coinciding with Louis's plans. He had no desire to see his sister reinstated as yet as Regent, for her captivity left him the leisure to establish himself as the arbiter of Savoy, with the Count of Bresse as his lieutenant-general. He consequently pretended to look upon the Duchess's emissary as a spy of the Duke of Burgundy; he declared that the ring which he recognised as his sister's had been stolen from her, and ordered Cavoretto to be arrested and thrown into prison.

Yolande, left without news of her messenger, and imagining in her ignorance that some evil had befallen him, resolved to make another effort to gain her brother's ear. This second envoy arrived at a moment when Claud de Seyssel had just come to the French Court on behalf of the

Three States to petition the King to assist them in obtaining Yolande's liberation. The King deemed it expedient this time to listen to the envoys' appeal, and he despatched a force of three hundred lances under Charles d'Amboise to bring about his sister's deliverance. On the night of October 2, 1476, by a strategic manœuvre, d'Amboise took possession of the Castle of Rouvre; the garrison was put to the sword, and the Duchess, with her children and her attendants, escaped on horseback to Tours, where King Louis came to meet her. His first words took the form of a sarcastic greeting: "Madame la Bourgogne, vous soyez la tres bien venue!" "She knew well," says Commines, "by his face that he was but joking; and replied very wisely that she was a good Frenchwoman, and ready to obey the King in all that he might command her. The said Lord conducted her to his chamber and treated her right royally."[1]

And another chronicler presents a picture of the familiar footing existing be-

[1] See Appendix.

tween this royal brother and sister in the following manner: "The King had his sister to sup with him and gave her many fair words and familiarities, calling her into his room when he went to bed and allowing her to warm for him his sheets and cushions, and to put him to bed, besides other services rendered to his Majesty: it was all of that most hearty familiarity which may exist between the most loving brother and sister." [1]

But the quaint homeliness of this family scene is somewhat marred by the mutual longing on the part of this "most loving brother and sister" to separate, and this is strongly set before us by Commines, who says: "True it is that he had great desire to be rid of her. She was very wise and was still keener to be gone, for they mutually knew each other well."

The King consequently urged the Duchess's departure in every way he could: he provided her with money; he engaged himself strictly to protect her states, her children, and herself against whatever foes

[1] See Appendix.

might assail them; while Yolande on her
side swore to enter into no alliance save
only with the King of France. The
brother and sister, having entered with all
solemnity into this covenant, parted, and
Yolande, having received from the King
many bits of stuff, both of silk and wool,
numerous jewels, together with her precious ring, started with all her children for
Chambéry, which she reached on December 9, 1476, in a downpour of rain and snow.

But Yolande's trials were not yet ended.
Her brother-in-law, the Count of Bresse,
refused to restore to her the government
of the Subalpine provinces, and not till
she was reinforced by an army, led in person by Galeazzo of Milan, did Philip
withdraw his claims and consent to acknowledge her supremacy.

"It was then, after so many struggles
and deceptions, that Yolande could rest
from the toils of life. Her mind had lost
none of its vigour; and she applied herself ardently to the relieving of her people.
The benefits of a wise administration shed
around her the blessings of a tardy peace :

she superintended the education of her family, left noble recollections of her Christian charity, visited the provinces. Many religious institutions bore witness to her piety. Never had the great qualities of this Princess made themselves felt in a more evident way. Her intellect was as young and active as ever." [1]

But her frame, never strong, was failing fast. The trials and anxieties she had undergone, the responsibilities that weighed on her from day to day, the shock of the murder of her brother-in-law, the Duke of Milan, and the death of the Duke of Burgundy at the battle of Nancy told severely on her, worn as she was with sickness and cares. The presentiment, too, that she would never recover from her illness was ever present with her, and hindered to a wide extent the possibility of coping successfully with the malady.

On August 10, 1478, she left Turin for the last time and repaired to Moncrivello for change of air.

[1] See Appendix.

Louis XI. and the widowed Duchess of
Milan sent messages of kindness and con-
dolence to Duchess Yolande on hearing
of her illness ; Louis, moved by remorse
for his former ill-treatment of his unfortunate sister, repeated his expressions of
kindness and protection to her son ; and
Duchess Bona sent for her relief her own
Court physician, who, however, arrived
too late, for on August 29, 1478, after
peacefully commending her soul to her
Maker, and her children and state to his
Most Christian Majesty the King of
France, Yolande of France, Duchess of
Savoy, passed calmly away, aged only
forty-four years.

The mortal remains of Duchess Yolande were laid to rest in the church at
Vercelli where her husband was buried ;
and the whole country mourned the loss
of her who " had been one of the most
virtuous and illustrious Princesses of her
time, who was marvellously attached to
the interests of the Crown of Savoy, and
who by her prudence and by her conduct
saved this state from the shipwreck which

threatened it during the illness of her husband and the minority of her son "[1]; and
"extraordinarily was she mourned by all
the people of Savoy."[2]

[1] Guichenon, *op. cit.*, ii., c. 28.   [2] *Ibid.*, *Histoire de Bresse.*

SHIELD OF YOLANDE OF FRANCE.

CHAPTER IV

BONA OF SAVOY. BROUGHT UP AT THE
COURT OF FRANCE. HER MARRIAGE
WITH THE DUKE OF MILAN, GALEAZZO
MARIA SFORZA. JOURNEY TO FLORENCE.
MURDER OF THE DUKE OF MILAN. BONA
NAMED REGENT OF THE STATE. HER
AMOURS. DEATH OF HER SON, GIAN GA-
LEAZZO, DUKE OF MILAN. BONA'S WITH-
DRAWAL TO FRANCE. HER POVERTY.
HER DEATH. (1449–1503.)

DURING the early part of the reign
of Louis XI. of France, the House
of Savoy—at least on the female side—
was well represented at his Court.

Louis's wife, Charlotte of Savoy, had
gathered around her three of her sisters,
two of whom quickly found husbands
in France. The eldest, Agnes, married
Francis of Orleans, Count of Dunois;
the younger one, Maria, married Francis,

BONA MA
RIA DVCIS
SA MLI·

BONA OF SAVOY, DUCHESS OF MILAN.

FROM A DRAWING MADE BY SIGNOR CESARE FERRARI FROM A MARBLE EFFIGY OF
BONA AT THE CERTOSA OF PAVIA.

Count of St. Pol, Constable of France.
All these sisters made their home at the
French Court, where Louis, out of love
for his wife, or from the consciousness of
the political advantages that he saw would
accrue to him from such a step, welcomed
his sisters-in-law.

But Bonne, or Bona (and as most of her
life was spent in Italy and among Italian
surroundings, she will be called by the
Italian version of her name), was an orphan when she came to France to be educated and disposed of according to the will
and choice of her brother-in-law.   Louis
was well aware of the value that a bride
of the loveliness and rank of Bona would
represent in his hands.   Of extraordinary
beauty, a Princess of the ancient House
of Savoy, and under the patronage of
the King of France, she was a prize that
might tempt many a wooer, while at the
same time the bestowal of her hand would
be a mark of the King's favour and a re-
compense to any fortunate suitor whom
his Majesty might wish to encourage or
reward.

The King was just then under special obligations to Francesco Sforza, Duke of Milan, the great *condottiere*, who had secured the hand of the heiress of the House of Visconti for himself, and who by his genius and energy had established himself on the throne of Milan. Francesco was anxious to continue in his dynasty the greatness of which he had laid the foundations; and by alliances, both matrimonial and civil, he bade fair to reach the goal of his ambition. Francesco's eldest son, Galeazzo, had gone, at his father's desire, to France at the head of a Milanese force to assist Louis against the " League for the Public Good," and so practical a form of friendship deserved a reward over and above that of merely fair words. The King knew well that a connection with his own royal house would be a compliment that Francesco Sforza, the grandson of the peasant of Cotignola, would appreciate, and he determined to bestow the hand of Bona of Savoy on Galeazzo Maria, the Heir Apparent to the Duchy of Milan.

But that this alliance should find favour with the bride's family was quite another matter. State reasons and family pride alike made the marriage an unpalatable one, and a great deal of opposition from several members of the House of Savoy was forthcoming on the occasion. But the sensitiveness of Amadeus IX. and his brothers had to give way before the resolution of Louis XI., and the marriage became a settled thing. The betrothal, however, did not take place till after the death of the Duke of Milan. When the news of this event reached Galeazzo he hurried off at once to Milan, where, owing to the prudence and firmness of his widowed mother, the Duchess Blanche, the succession was secured to him. Galeazzo made a sorry return to his mother in after years for the devotion she had displayed on his behalf, for, after enduring persecutions, neglect, and cruelty from him, she died at the age of forty-two. Her death, according to Corio,[1] was "due more to poison than to natural infirmity." In that

---

[1] Corio, *Storia di Milano*, Prima Edizione.

death rumour has it that her son had no small share; he never cleared himself.

The betrothal of the affianced pair took place at the Castle of Ambois, when Tristan Sforza, the Duke's natural brother, was proxy for the bridegroom. After the ceremony he wrote a long despatch to the Duke, telling him of all the incidents that had occurred. He describes the long procession of lords and ladies, of the princes of the blood, of the Queen and her suite, and of the King, who led in the bride, holding her by the right hand. He minutely pictures the ceremonial when the King placed the nuptial ring on Bona's finger; he goes on to say that a solemn mass was celebrated, after which the blessing was given; and then that he bestowed on "Vostra Illustrissima Consorte" the kiss of peace, seeing that such was the custom. The bride's dress he describes as follows: "The above mentioned, your Consort, was dressed in regal fashion in a robe of white cloth of gold, having the royal crown on her head with many, great, and precious ornaments; her hair was spread over her shoulders as is customary here at such weddings, which was constantly handled and set in order by His afore-mentioned Majesty together with many jocund and pleasant words."[1]

The wedding service being ended, their Majesties, the bride and the proxy bridegroom, Tristan, retired to the King's own rooms, where Tristan presented on Duke Galeazzo's behalf the jewels sent by him to Bona, and which evidently caused great satisfaction. "I presented her first of all with the little ring with a heart whose signification I begged her to note ; then I gave the buckles ; then the necklace, the sight of which caused Their Majesties to marvel, for not only did they admire it greatly but they extolled it above measure. The King among other words spake also these : ' I thank your dear brother for such beautiful jewels ' ; whereupon I replied that Your Highness would give even better ones, whereat he said he well knew

[1] Letter to Galeazzo Maria, Duke of Milan, from Tristan Sforza, 1468. From Marchele Felice di San Tommalo's *Notizie intorno alla Vita di Bona di Savoia*, Torino, 1838 (Bocca).

the love he bore him, and how mighty and magnanimous he was, with other fair and pleasant words, while all the time the jewels were now in the hands of His Majesty the King, now in those of Her Majesty the Queen, who then with my help put them on her [Bona], round her neck, on her shoulders, on her head, on her arms. Finally all the company went upstairs to a hall where feasting and dancing occupied the rest of the day." The honours shown to the Duke's representative were said to have been out of the common and of a nature that Louis XI. did not generally exhibit to his guests ; but they do not seem to have had the effect of making Tristan desirous to prolong his stay in France, for he inserts a postscript in his letter to his brother in which he says : "If I should remain in this country, *which God forbid*, I would employ a cypher," a hint that he was aware of the treachery reigning around him, and of the need of guarding against any double-dealing whereby the interests of the Milanese Court might be injuriously affected.

A few days after the betrothal, Tristan
set out to escort the bride to her new
home and present her to her husband.
Great care was taken in selecting the
route whereby they were to travel; any
Savoyard territory was carefully avoided,
probably from the dread lest some of her
family might kidnap the bride, and prevent the marriage from being carried out.
This would not have been the first time
that such a high-handed proceeding
had been resorted to by those princes.
There was a suspicion that the House
of Savoy, in an endeavour to secure the
Duchy of Milan, had attempted a similar
move on the occasion of Galeazzo's return
from France at the moment of his father's
death; and that after two days' confinement in the Duke of Savoy's territory he
had escaped, owing to the devotion of one
of his servitors who baffled the vigilance
of Galeazzo's keepers and saved his master from the trap laid for him by Yolande,
Duchess of Savoy.

The bridal party travelled by way of
Marseilles and Genoa, and the marriage

between Galeazzo and Bona was celebrated at Pavia on the 6th of July, 1468.

Three years later the Duke and Duchess travelled to Florence, when the pomp with which they journeyed excited the attention of high and low. Duke Galeazzo had a love of display only equalled by his cruelty and vice, and he spared no expense to make his visit to Florence the occasion for an outlay and magnificence such as the richest monarch of modern days would not dream of emulating.

" The chief vassals and councillors of the Duke went with him in suits of clothes laden with gold and silver, each one being in his turn accompanied by servitors sumptuously apparelled. The Ducal pensioners were all clothed in velvet. Forty waiting-men were decorated with superb chains of gold round their necks. Other waiting-men had embroidered suits. The Duke's grooms were in silk liveries faced with silver. For the Duchess fifty steeds were set apart and ready with their saddles on, their trappings being all of gold and silver ; her pages were richly dressed ; she had twelve chariots all covered with cloth of gold and silver and embroidered with the ducal arms; the mattresses and feather-beds inside were of cloth with costly lace (*rizzo sopra rizzo*); some were of silver, others of crimson satin, and even the trappings of her horses were covered with silk. There followed in the ducal train fifty steeds with saddles of cloth of gold, and silver stirrups; fifty men-at-arms, each so magnificent that he might have been a captain, five hundred picked soldiers; one hundred mules covered with the richest embroidered cloth of gold; three thousand horses and also two hundred mules covered alike in damask for the transport of the courtiers."[1] The procession was finally brought to a close by five hundred couples of hounds, and an unheard-of number of falcons, sparrow-hawks, trumpeters, musicians, and jugglers, who were all conveyed across the Apennines to the inconvenience and dismay, it may be supposed, of those who would have to lodge and board them in " Arno's fair white walls "!

[1] Corio, *op. cit.*, p. 4.

The cortège returned by Lucca and Genoa, and at both places Bona was presented with gifts, Lucca offering her two white geldings and ten thousand ducats, while Genoa presented her with many silk hangings for her rooms and some silk brocades.

Soon after the return of the Duke and Duchess to Milan, Bona's second child, Bianca Maria, was born, and not long after that, again, great festivities were held in honour of the betrothal of Gian Galeazzo, the Duke's eldest son, aged four years, to Isabella of Aragon, the daughter of Alfonso, Duke of Calabria, and Ippolita Sforza; and two years later, Philibert of Savoy was affianced to little Bianca Maria, who had reached the age of two.

But these bright matrimonial prospects were about to be darkened by the tragedy of the Duke's death. Galeazzo was a man, or rather a monster, whose cruelties, vices, and evil passions had excited the rage, disgust, and hatred of his subjects. His mania for hunting made him act at times in a manner so brutal as to be almost in-

credible, and but one instance will suffice
to show what form his anger could take
if, in any way, his game-laws were in-
fringed. A peasant had killed a hare.
This was in direct disobedience to the
orders of the Duke, who wreaked his
vengeance upon him. He condemned the
wretched man to swallow the hare, raw,
together with its skin, hair and all, and—
it need hardly be added—the man died in
agony.

Besides the Duke's cruelty and immor-
ality, he oppressed his subjects with numerous and heavy taxes, and the fate that
overtook him at last may by no means be
considered undeserved. A conspiracy was
formed against him, and on St. Stephen's
Day, while assisting at Mass in the church
of that name, he was stabbed by three
Milanese youths, who hoped that on the
tyrant's death all the citizens would rise
against his dynasty and assert their freedom and independence.

Galeazzo had had many presentiments
as to his end, and before leaving home
to go to the church he took leave of his

children (with whom he had kept with much solemnity all the Christmas festivities) as though he was never to see them again.

His corpse was exposed in the Chapter of the church where he had met his end; and Bona sent three rings and a seal of great price to be placed in the coffin of her youthful husband (for he was but thirty-three at the time of his death), together with a suit of white cloth in which Galeazzo had always expressed a wish to be buried.

The hopes of the conspirators that the whole town would rise and throw off the ducal yoke were not fulfilled. The Milanese quietly consented to the succession of the Duke's little son, Gian Galeazzo; but as he was only seven years of age his mother, Bona, was appointed Regent and guardian. Francesco (Cicho) Simonetta was named her chief councillor and director.

The difficulties that Bona had to encounter in her capacity as Regent may to some extent be compared with those un-

dergone about this same date in Savoy
by her sister-in-law, Yolande of France.
Both women had opposed to them a set of
brothers-in-law full of ambition, craft, and
audacity; both also had powerful neighbours to conciliate or repel; and both
were young and beautiful women. But
there the resemblance ceases; for the
characters of these Regents were as different as possible. Yolande was irreproach-
able in her morals, and gifted besides with
intellectual powers of a greatly superior
nature to those of her sister-in-law. Bona,
on the other hand, was a woman of low
tastes and habits. Her behaviour was im-
moral and undignified. Her conduct had
the most disastrous results, not only for the
family of Sforza but for the whole of
Italy as well.

There was at that moment at the Court
of Milan a certain Antonio Tassino, who
had come from Ferrara in the capacity of
merchant, and who had then entered the
ducal service, being appointed by Galeazzo
himself to wait specially on the Duchess.
This man, who was extraordinarily hand-

some, gained a complete ascendancy over Duchess Bona. She fell hopelessly in love with him, confided to him all the state secrets and, in spite of the warnings of her upright and wise minister, Simonetta, she trusted him blindly. This man knew well that Simonetta had neither esteem nor liking for him, and the knowledge of this dislike prompted Tassino to vengeance. He threw himself into the party of Lodovico Sforza, the cleverest and most ambitious of the late Duke's brothers, and Lodovico knew well how to make use of such a tool. Through Tassino's instrumentality Lodovico was reinstated in office and readmitted into the town of Milan, from which he had been wisely removed by the advice of Simonetta. In vain the minister warned Bona against the folly of such a step; she refused to listen to any counsel that seemed to her antagonistic to her lover. Simonetta's prophetic words on Lodovico's entry into the town, "I shall lose my head, and you, the state," were uttered in vain. The prophecy, however, was but too quickly fulfilled.

Hardly was Lodovico back in Milan before he caused Simonetta to be arrested and soon after beheaded. He then named himself tutor to his young nephew, and removed Bona from her share in the government, bidding her "to attend rather to her devotions than to the sovereignty of the state." From that time forward Lodovico the Moor was absolute master of Milan. He banished Tassino, whose insolence and vanity procured him enemies on all sides ; and the favourite, laden with jewels and treasure, retired to Venice. Duchess Bona was wild at this exile of her lover : her desire to rejoin him became her ruling idea, and made her alike oblivious of her duties as a mother and of her dignity as a woman. In order to carry out her folly, she consented to renounce publicly and voluntarily all share in the government of her son's state, hoping by such a step to be free from all responsibility, and at liberty to set off to rejoin Tassino.

But the crafty Lodovico had other aims in his head. He had no intention that

Bona should leave the duchy, as, when once out of the country, he feared she would but too easily and readily find friends and relatives to espouse her cause and to reinstate her in power. He consequently took all necessary measures to prevent her departure, detaining her for a long time in a sort of honourable captivity, and surrounding her always with creatures of his own appointing. Poor Duchess Bona, deprived of her high office, and baffled in her intention to find compensation for such a loss in the arms of her lover, presents a sorry figure.

The crown of sorrows, though, awaited her in 1494, when her son, Gian Galeazzo, who had reigned as a puppet in his uncle's hands, died at the Castle of Pavia ; the cause of his death was slow poison, which it is generally supposed was administered to him by Lodovico's orders. Bona was allowed by her despotic brother-in-law to attend on her son in his last illness. Who can tell but that the bitterest drop in her cup of agony was caused by the reflection that his life might have been spared, had she only stayed at the head of affairs, and not given up "her all on earth and more than all in Heaven" for a wretch quite unworthy of such love and sacrifice.

After her son's death Bona was allowed to withdraw to France, where her life was of so retired a nature as to induce some writers to believe that she died in 1499. But recent discoveries have proved clearly that she was living in 1502 at the Castle of Fossano, situated in the lands of her nephew, Philibert II. of Savoy, and that she died there in the second half of November, 1503. It is piteous to read of the straits in money matters to which she was reduced, and to know that her latter years were harassed with the ceaseless struggle to obtain her rightful income. How often the reflection of the wealth she once possessed must have forced itself upon her when she was inditing letters imploring for the means " de satisfaire à mes premières nécessités!" And how bitter then must have been the remembrance of the treasures that once were hers before assassination had left her house desolate!

The place of Duchess Bona's sepulture is uncertain. Complete mystery surrounds the last hours of one whose existence is a record of sin and folly, though touched at every point by the sanctifying hand of sorrow and misfortune.

SEAL OF COUNT AYMON OF SAVOY.

Carolus I Dux Amedei filius, Philiberti frater, Sabaudiæ
Dux V. Cypri Rex, à Beroldo XXIII. natus Cariuani die 29.
Martij Anno 1468. Blanchæ Ferratensi junctus omnia de
jure Cypri à Carlottâ ejus Materterâ concessa suscepit Cameranum,
Mommajorem Comites, et aliquot alios Proceres, qui nouaue =
rant compressit. Salutarumque Marchionem causâ cognitâ
feudo priuauit. Arce Nicenâ turribus, et propugnaculis munitâ,
controuersias cum Carolo Francorum Rege ad Pontem Belin =
cineum transactione diremit. De Litteris, et litteratis benemeri =
tus formâ, viribus, et animi dotibus præstitit. Occubuit Pinarolij
die 13ª Martij, Anno 1490.

CHAPTER V

BLANCHE OF MONTFERRAT. HER MARRIAGE
WITH DUKE CHARLES I. OF SAVOY. HIS
DEATH. BLANCHE'S REGENCY. THE CHEV-
ALIER BAYARD. ARRIVAL OF CHARLES
VIII. OF FRANCE IN ITALY. HIS RECEP-
TION IN TURIN. DEATH OF THE YOUNG
DUKE. BLANCHE'S LIFE AT CARIGNAN.
BAYARD'S TOURNEY. HER DEATH. (1485–
1519.)

ON the night of the 1st of April,
1485, an august company was
assembled in the hall of audience in the
Castle of Casale. The hour was near two
o'clock in the morning, and the occasion
was the betrothal of Blanche of Montferrat to Charles I., surnamed "the Warrior," Duke of Savoy. The chief figure
in that assembly was Boniface, Marquis
of Montferrat. He was a man old in
years, but renowned as one of the greatest

warriors of his day ; following in the foot-
steps of many of his ancestors, he had
gained renown as a *condottiere*, and
had served as general to the forces of
Venice, the Visconti, and the Sforza when
they had summoned him on different occasions to lead their armies to battle.
Called on to succeed two brothers who
had filled successively the Marquisate of
Montferrat, Boniface applied himself to
the new duties devolving on him. These
included the office of guardian to his or-
phaned nieces, the daughters of his brother,
the Marquis William.

William's career had been that of a regu-
lar soldier of fortune. Francesco Sforza—
no mean judge of fighting and fighters—
had pronounced him to be the ablest
captain in Italy. He had been married
three times. His hopes, however, of continuing the dynasty in his own male descendants had proved illusive. He had
not resorted to wedlock until considerably
advanced in years. So Providence, to
punish him for not having availed himself
of the privilege of matrimony when young,

had bestowed on him two female children, Jane, or Joanna, the daughter of his first wife, Marie de Foix ; and Blanche, by his second wife, Elisabetta Maria Sforza, the daughter of Francesco Sforza, Duke of Milan. This second wife was only thirteen years old when she became the bride of William of Montferrat ; and it can only be hoped that she was too young and too ignorant to shudder at the fate which allied her to a bridegroom of sixty-five, as the chronicles of Montferrat assert the age of the Marquis to have been. But, all the same, he outlived this second wife, married a third one, and died in 1483, leaving his brother Boniface to inherit his dignities, and to succeed, if possible, where he had failed in providing a son to carry on the family honours.

Boniface hastened to try to accomplish all that was required of him. Though a bachelor, and an old one into the bargain, he lost no time in marrying Hélène de Brosse, the sister of his brother's third wife ; but at first no better fate attended him than had befallen the late Marquis.   A daughter was the only issue of this marriage, prompted entirely by diplomacy, and not in the least by inclination.   The succession of Montferrat became, therefore, a burning question. All the neighbouring states had parcelled out his heritage to suit their respective requirements and ambitions before Marquis Boniface had left off thinking of brides and children.

The eldest daughter of Marquis William had thought of securing to herself and to her husband, the Marquis de Saluces, the succession after her father's death; for a stipulation in her marriage-contract had insured this right to her, provided that Boniface had no son.   She, for her part, undertook to hand over a handsome marriage-portion to her half-sister Blanche when the moment came for her to be married.

The most powerful claimants after Joanna and her husband were Lodovico Sforza, Duke of Bari (surnamed the Moor), and the Duke of Savoy.   The latter, whose family had already contracted several alliances with the House of Mont-

ferrat, based his claim on the relationships
resulting from these marriages; his ap-
proaching union with Blanche strengthened his pretensions, and in order to
enforce them still further the Duke resolved to be married without any more
delay.   He was seconded in this resolution by Lodovico the Moor, who, with all
the cunning and sagacity which he possessed in so remarkable a degree, determined to go shares with Savoy in the
division of Montferrat, to the utter exclusion of the Marquis de Saluces and his
wife.   The contract was drawn up in all
haste at Casale (Duke Charles being represented by his emissary, Antoine de la
Fôret), when it was decided that Blanche
should receive a marriage-portion of eighty
thousand ducats; or, should she have no
male cousin to succeed to her uncle's estates, she was then to " inherit all the lands,
rights, and jurisdictions situate beyond the
Po," and the vassals, chatelains, and people of those lands were to swear to observe this covenant, and to yield obedience
to Savoy without further objection.

The marriage was contracted in the manner known as *sponsalia per verba de præsenti* (a form done away with by the Council of Trent), and the young couple only awaited the moment of meeting to perform the rite with the full ceremonial enjoined by the Church, and befitting their exalted position.

But the wary old Marquis had no idea of calmly letting his patrimony go away into different ramifications of nieces and nephews-in-law. He, too, had his schemes —he, too, had visions of brides and sons ; and in spite of his advanced age he, too, was about to become again a bridegroom. The calculating relatives probably laughed at Boniface's dreams and doings ; but the laughter must have died away on their lips when, in due time, his second wife, Mary of Servia, bore him two sons, and the longed-for possession of Montferrat became, for the House of Savoy, a prize to dream of and to struggle after. It was two centuries later when, after possession by the Marquis of Mantua, it became Savoyan territory.

But apart from the plots and counter-plots for the succession of Montferrat, Duke Charles of Savoy was eager for the arrival of his bride ; the reports of her beauty, of her goodness, and her intelligence made him anxious to behold her, and while awaiting her presence he did his utmost to prepare for her reception, and to secure the papal dispensation needed to make them lawful husband and wife.[1] Fifty archers of the Guard were to form the Duchess's escort ; a tailor, Pierre Roche, was to be in attendance to fashion new and smart wearing apparel for the bride ; and, with even still greater consideration, a cook was despatched from the ducal establishment to preside over the travelling kitchen of the Duchess Blanche.   Truly a bridegroom who showed such care, not only for the wearing apparel of his bride, but also for the exigencies of her table, bade fair to make a model husband.

[1] Usseglio, L. *Bianca di Montferrato*, Cap. I., p. 17, Roux e Ca., Torino, 1892. Charles I.'s grandfather, Lodovico of Savoy, and Blanche's maternal grandmother, Jane or Joanna, were brother and sister ; the affianced pair were therefore second cousins.

While sending forward these emissaries on the road, the Duke busied himself at Turin in preparing a stupendous quantity of dresses of velvet, satin, and cloth of gold for himself, his brother, the Marquis of Gex, and the whole Court ; after which he removed to Moncrivello, and from there to Crescentino, where his bride met him, followed by a numerous train of councillors, ladies-in-waiting, shield-bearers, doctors, astrologers, and retainers of all sorts and kinds, who were lodged and boarded for several days by the Duke at Moncrivello, where all awaited the longed-for dispensation from Rome. This arrived, at last, on May 9, 1484, and two days after, in the presence of all the grandees of his Court, his uncle Francis, Archbishop of Auch; his brother Giacomo Luigi ; Gabriel de Seyssel, Lord of Aix ; Enrico de Valperga, majordomo of the palace, and many others, the Duke declared that his marriage with Blanche of Montferrat, contracted in his name by his proxy, Antoine de la Fôret, was now valid and consummated, owing to the papal dispensation, without which their marriage could not have received the blessing and sanction of the Church. The bride was not present at this ceremony, but the nuptials having been blessed and ratified by the Pope, no further function was required and the young couple were lawfully joined together from that moment, all the requirements of church and state having been satisfied.

Five days were spent at Moncrivello, and were devoted to preparations for the solemn entry into Turin, which took place on the afternoon of the 19th, after one night's halt at Chivasso. The brilliant cavalcade, having arrived at the capital, found shelter in the principal inns, for the Castle and the Episcopal Palace retained for the use of the guests were not sufficient to house all the cortège of barons and nobles who flocked from Savoy and Montferrat to do honour to the newly married pair. The reception accorded them by the town of Turin was hearty and effusive ; and the wonderful beauty of Blanche, her charm of manner, and her intellectual gifts attracted and fascinated all classes of her husband's subjects. Feastings, entertainments, illuminations, and other demonstrations evinced the public joy, and rich and poor alike did all that lay in their power to testify their satisfaction in their Prince's nuptials and to welcome his fair young bride.

This bright opening of a life whose happiness was to be all too short-lived was clouded over by the death of the Duke's young brother, Giacomo Luigi, Marquis of Gex. The lad, for he was but about fifteen at the time of his death, had always been delicate, and the frequent bills from the apothecary show how efforts were constantly made to restore the boy's health. The Duke, whose love for this delicate brother was very great, had spent large sums in many of the churches of Turin for votive offerings, hoping in this way to bring about his brother's restoration to health; but in July of this same year (1485) he became so much worse that all hopes of his recovery were at an end. No remedies availed to save the

young, dearly loved life : the skill of num-
berless doctors proved useless, a bath of
oil administered on the last day of the
youth's life failed to restore him to his devoted brother, and on the 17th of the
month he died.   A costly funeral was held
in his honour in the Church of St. John,
and he was interred with every possible
mark of pomp and respect before the high
altar, all the clergy of the town assisting
at the mass for the repose of his soul.

After the sad ceremony was finished, the
Duke and Duchess, to escape for a while
from the mournful associations surrounding them, left Turin for Rivoli, where they
passed the rest of the summer.   A further
journey was planned later on in the year,
to show the Duchess her husband's country, and to introduce her to the beauty of
her new surroundings.   A journey to Savoy was decided upon, and preparations
for the undertaking were set on foot.   The
removal of the Court from one place to
another was no small affair in those days,
the more so when it was also a question
of crossing the Alps, when the amount of

luggage alone required a special service, including as it did the hangings and tapestries that the Duke conveyed from one house to another to cover the bare walls, and extending to the Duchess's pet parrot and sparrow, who had also to be calculated for in the removal. There were, besides, heaps of kitchen utensils, tools, plate, arms, and clothes to be transported, and the number of pack-horses and mules that were needed on these occasions was simply interminable. This caravan was followed by a host of courtiers, gentlemen- and ladies-in-waiting, squires, valets, and waiting-men, so that the removal of the Court seemed like the march of a whole army, and involved no end of organisation and expense. All the same, the time devoted to these journeys was shorter than might have been imagined. This one, which was taken leisurely, occupied only seventeen days, starting from Rivoli on the 26th of September and reaching Geneva on the 12th of October, after crossing the Mont Cenis and halting at Susa, Aiguebelle, and Annecy. The Duchess

was carried in a litter, although, with unheard-of luxury for those times, a coach had
been prepared for her, decorated with the
arms of Savoy and Montferrat, and adorned
with much painting and gilding — an
elaborate piece of work, in sooth, that had
engrossed the labours of the painter, one
Georges Jaquier, for no less than three
months. There was also a palfrey in readiness for the Duchess, led by her squires,
so that she could vary her mode of progress
in divers ways should she wish to do so.

Duke Charles and Duchess Blanche
stayed for three months at Geneva, and
the whole of their stay was one long succession of feasts and amusements. There
were boar-hunts; there were expeditions
on the lake, pantomimes, theatrical per-
formances, grand Church functions, visits
from the Duke's sister Maria and her husband, the Marquis de Kochberg, and other
innocent pastimes wherewith to gladden
the hearts and enliven the spirits of the
young couple.

Geneva was the place chosen for gaiety
and festivity; while Chambéry, on the

other hand, was set apart for the more solemn season of Lent. The Duke and his bride left the lovely Lake Leman at the end of January and reached the capital of Savoy the 4th of February, where they observed Lent very strictly; the Duke, on Holy Thursday, revived a custom that had fallen into neglect for some years in the House of Savoy—of feeding and waiting on thirteen old men, and washing their feet on his knees. After Easter, they returned to Piedmont, where disputes and negotiations between Savoy and Saluces (involving also unpleasant relations with France) occupied the attention of the Duke, and plunged him finally into a war with Lodovico, Marquis of Saluces. The Duke, whose delight in war was a well-known fact, was repeatedly successful in this campaign; but his devotion to his young wife made him unselfishly give up his favourite pursuit to be near Blanche, whose confinement was not far distant. For three months Charles stayed with his Duchess at Turin; and on the 11th of July, 1487, Blanche was safely delivered of a daughter. The child, over whose birth great rejoicings were held, may be said literally to have been cradled in gold, for a magnificent cot had been prepared for her in Milan, chiselled by the hand of Lodovico Casano, and edged with an elaborate bit of carving representing the nativity of Christ, with devices of the arms of Savoy, Montferrat, and other great families allied to them, painted and gilded by one Giovanni Ambrosio. The coverlet was a rich piece of cloth of gold lined with no less than 342 skins of ermine ; and the price of this princely cradle was reckoned at about 830 florins. The infant was baptised in the Cathedral Church of St. John on Sunday, July 29th, and two godmothers and five godfathers acted as her sponsors. They were : Maria, Marchesa of Montferrat ; the Lady Paola Gambara, wife of Lodovico Costa, Lord of Bene ; Lodovico Sforza, Duke of Bari (who was represented by Galeazzo Visconti with a following of twenty-four horse); Urban of Bonnivard, Bishop of Vercelli ; Jean Compeys, Archbishop of Tarantasia ;

Antoine Champion, Bishop of Mondovi and Chancellor of Savoy ; and Agostino de Corradidi Lignana, Abbot of Casanova. The festivities in honour of the christening were on such an extensive scale that even the sumptuous amount of plate owned by the Duke was not sufficient for the use of his guests, and he had to borrow from his brother, Count Giano of Savoy, from the Count de la Chambre, from the Countess Valperga, and from the Canon of Vercelli to make good the deficiency.

The next event that marks the life of Blanche was the birth of a son, on June 3, 1488. The Duke had gone to France in the previous month of March, to see if, by a personal interview with his royal cousin, he could not smooth away the difficulties and disagreements on the question of the homage owed by the Marquis of Saluces to the Duke of Savoy. Charles had gone with a retinue of over a thousand men, and, regardless of the ever-failing condition of his exchequer, had determined on a display of riches and

magnificence, trusting that this appearance
of wealth would mislead King Charles
VIII. as to the state of his finances, and
persuade him of the futility of waging war
against an adversary whose funds and
supplies were evidently inexhaustible.
But the King of France was either better
informed as to the state of his cousin's
exchequer, or was not to be deceived by
the trick practised upon him; he held out
against the Duke's arguments; he supported the claims of Saluces as opposed
to those of Savoy; and the Duke had to
come away, after having expended vast
sums and reaped few of the benefits that
he had promised himself in return for this
outlay of time and money.   Before leaving France the news reached him of the
birth of a son, and he instantly besought
the French monarch to stand godfather
to his boy, a request to which Charles
VIII. at once acceded.

During the absence of her husband
Duchess Blanche had remained at Turin,
leading a quiet, retired life, occupied with
her handmaidens in embroidery, as well

as other housewifely pursuits, attending
Mass frequently, and devoted also to
alms-giving. The only amusement she
allowed herself was a concert in the last
days of Carnival; and after this one outburst of musical dissipation all sounds of
revelry were exchanged for the sermons
of Father Angelo da Chivasso, who had
the honour of preaching to the Duchess
and her Court during Lent. These pious
observances were varied with the preparations made for Blanche's confinement;
and in a beautiful large chamber, all hung
with red and white satin, she gave birth to
her first-born son on the morning of June
23, 1489. The event was hailed with en-
thusiasm and delight in Turin; couriers
rushed in all directions to proclaim the
news; guns were fired; fireworks were
shot off; bands of music patrolled the
streets to proclaim the birth of an heir to
the throne. The Prince's baptism was
fixed for the 2d of August, so that the
sponsors or their representatives might
have time to arrive for the ceremony;
while festivities, consisting chiefly of music,

singing, and dancing were inaugurated at Court in honour of the event.

On Sunday, August 2d, the baptism took place. The whole Court issued from the castle and proceeded in great state to the cathedral. The street through which the cortège passed was strewn with leaves and flowers; great branches from the trees gave a grateful shade on either side of the road. The church was hung with silks and brocades, and shone with thousands of wax candles, which glistened "like the sun and the moon"; while to do honour to the baby-prince innumerable sacred relics were displayed throughout the building. The procession was met by the bishops and clergy, and then moved along the cathedral to the sound of chanting and hymns, after which the ceremony was performed in the ducal chapel. The babe received three names : Charles, out of compliment to his godfather, the King of France ; John, because he was born on the vigil of St. John's Day ; and Amadeus, in memory of his grandfather, Amadeus VIII. The Duke was not present at his son's christening ; he had tarried at Chambéry on his way from France, and from there he went to join the Duchess at Turin, where he was received with exuberant demonstrations of delight and affection on the part of his subjects.

But besides the political failure of his French expedition, Charles did not return in the same conditions physically as those in which he had started. His health, never very robust, gave signs of failing, and his physicians, perplexed at the symptoms, suggested change of air. The Duke refused to be frightened by disease. He fought against the evil with all the energy and courage of his nature, exerting himself to attend to his multiform duties notwithstanding the increasing languor and weakness which sapped his strength and vitality. He followed, however, the advice given him, and journeyed first to Moncalieri, then to Pinerolo, where much was hoped from the salubriousness of the air. But he was a doomed man. One doctor after another was called in, only to make a vain trial of his skill, and to pro-

VIEW OF CASALE.

nounce himself incompetent to save the
Duke's life.   It would be tedious, were it
not pathetic, to read in turn the names of
the different physicians as they passed in
endless file by the dying man's bedside,
each one trying some new medicine and
subjecting the patient—uselessly—to fresh
examinations   and   fresh   prescriptions.
"No medicine in the world can do thee
good," for here, as of old with "Hamlet the
Dane," the case was one of poisoning, and
no remedy was forthcoming to counteract
the subtle disease.   The Duchess made
votive offerings for the life of her youthful husband ; an image in wax whose
weight was equal to that of the Duke was
offered up by her at the Church of "Nos-
tro Signore della Misericordia" at Ales-
sandria.   Prayers and intercessions and
vows were all in vain, and on March 14,
1490, Duke Charles the Warrior died.
Had he lived another eleven days he
would only then have attained the age of
twenty-two.

The lamentations over his premature
death were genuine and universal.   His

talents, his activity, his zeal for his country's good, had raised the fondest hopes
concerning him. The people, who were still
suffering from the weakness of Louis's
reign, from the unsettled minority of Philibert, and the turbulence consequent on the
regency of Yolande of France, had seen
in the accession of Charles I. the likelihood
of a wise and firm rule, the consolidation of
the ducal dynasty, and a long prospect
of peace and prosperity. Now all these
visions were forever destroyed.   The
Duke's heir was a babe of nine months,
and a minority and regency, even though
watched over by the care and wisdom of
Blanche, were overshadowed by the probability of dissensions and disturbances at the
hands of Philip de Bresse.

> " Well indeed might they be shaken
>   With the weight of such a blow ;
> He was gone—their prince, their idol,
>   Whom they loved and worshipped so ! " [1]

The rumour that Charles had been poi-
soned was first raised by the tribe of phy-

[1] Aytoun, *Lays of the Scottish Cavaliers.*

sicians whose skill had been baffled by the
Duke's illness, and who sought to excuse
their incompetence by alleging an evil beyond the control of human agency. The
guilt of this crime was ascribed to the
Marquis de Saluces, whose hatred of Duke
Charles was well known, and who was also
accused of compassing in the same way,
and at about the same time, the deaths of
the Marshal de Miolans, and of a member
of the Fieschi family, who were both bitter enemies of the Marquis and warm
adherents of the Duke. Some milder
judgments, though, exonerate the Marquis
from so foul a crime, and point to the delicacy of all the children of Duke Amadeus
IX. and Yolande of France, and to the
demands made on his strength and youth
before Charles was old enough to endure
them.

The funeral honours bestowed upon
Charles I. were lavish in the extreme.
The number of torches burnt, of masses
chanted, of priests and people who
thronged to attend the rites, all testify to
the love and respect which were now

poured forth as the last tribute of a nation's grief and homage. The body, wrapped in a large scarlet mantle trimmed with ermine, a cap of red velvet on the head, was borne to the ducal chapel, where it lay in state for three days. During this time constant Masses were said; day and night the brothers of the five convents of Pinerolo stood round the bier chanting the prayers for the dead. On the 18th of March the funeral took place. The body, which had been embalmed, was carried to the Church of St. Francis, and there immured. The church was all hung in black, and thousands of wax candles, supplied from every part of Piedmont—as those of Pinerolo were not nearly sufficient for the purpose—relieved the darkness of the funeral hangings. The bier was escorted by an immense concourse of people, prelates, clerks, nobles, and poor people (the latter all clad in mourning provided by the Court), carrying torches on which were stamped the arms of Savoy, while all the bells in the town and the neighbourhood tolled out sadly and slowly their tale

of death and mourning.   After the body
had been laid in its last resting-place, the
Bishops of Mondovì, of Vercelli, and of
Moriana officiated separately at a solemn
Mass.   No less than three hundred and
nine Masses were said that very morning
in the same church by priests summoned
for the purpose from far and near.   Funeral services and functions lasted after
this for nine days.   During those days of
mourning and weeping, alms were also
given to nearly three thousand poor
people.

What words, though, can describe the
grief of the Duchess Blanche at the death
of her young and beloved husband? Her
sorrow was profound and lasting.   The
weeds, which she assumed then and never
entirely put off, were but outward tokens
of the desolation which entered her heart,
never again to leave it altogether on this
side of the grave.   The mourning observed
at Court was also deep and genuine.   The
rooms were all draped in black ; and that
every member of the household also wore
sables it is hardly necessary to say.

But the relief, the luxury, as it were, of indulging in her grief, the solace of dwelling on the memories of her happy past undisturbed by state cares and anxieties, was a privilege altogether impossible for the Duchess. Her thoughts and interests had to be wholly devoted to the administration of the government, to the bringing up of her children, although the sympathy, the advice, and the companionship, which would have turned her task into a pleasure, had gone from beside her and was replaced only by an utter void in all its novelty and bitterness. The mortal remains of Charles I. were hardly laid to rest ere his vassals thronged around his widow to renew their oath of allegiance; state officers entreated for a confirmation in her son's name of their different employments; councillors applied for instructions; her subjects implored her clemency and protection; and Blanche, forcing back thoughts that might now find no place in her mind, and tears which might no longer flow, let none go away unsatisfied. She exerted herself, with a diligence and an

energy beyond her years, to inspire her
people with confidence and courage, and
to convince them that all was not lost in
the death of their sovereign.

The question as to the Regency and the
guardianship of the young Duke engrossed
all minds.   No doubt was entertained that
the great-uncles of the child (especially
the restless and ambitious Philip de Bresse)
would leave no stone unturned to possess
themselves of the person of Charles II.,
and of the reins of office.   But Blanche
was determined that no one but herself
should bring up her child, or rule in his
name.   She knew how keen a struggle
such a determination would involve, and
she resolved to lose no time in taking the
necessary measures to insure her nomination both as guardian and as Regent.   She
was backed in her resolution by Monsignor Francis of Savoy, the only one of
her husband's uncles who had no wish to
usurp his great-nephew's rights, and who,
having spent much of his time with Charles
and Blanche, was really fond of his relatives.   He had always warmly espoused

Blanche's side in all her troubles and per-
plexities.   Supported by him, the Duchess
called together her Council, and announced
to them her desire to hear their opinions
and wishes as to her son's guardianship.
But one voice reigned throughout the assembly, and the councillors all declared
that, owing to her exceptional gifts, her
love of justice tempered with mercy, her
virtue, her intellect, and her prudence,
Blanche of Montferrat, and she alone, was
fit to rule over the person and over the
state of her infant son.   This office the
Duchess accepted at once ; she swore on
the Gospel to rule well and faithfully ; and
she then and there appointed Monsignor
Francis as Governor-General under her.

And sore was the need in which Blanche
stood of a firm and friendly adviser at
that moment.   The war with Saluces still
continued, fomented through several gen-
erations by hatred and jealousy, and un-
dermining by its continuance the strength
of both states.   The attitude adopted by
Philip de Bresse presented a greater
peril still, in the shape of civil war.   The

exchequer was empty, drained to its last
farthing by Duke Charles's expedition
into France. The effect of these unto-
ward circumstances made itself felt in an
agitation and irresolution in the minds of
the Duchess's subjects which boded ill in
the face of a civil war. But through this
trying time Blanche gave no sign of
either weakness or wavering. Though
accustomed to a life centred in home
duties and home interests, with no training for public life or its responsibilities,
she rose to her position with all the energy
and resolution of a great mind, and her behaviour throughout this critical period was
guided by the promptings of genius. No
symptom of yielding encouraged the sedi-
tious spirits to come to the front. Even
the dauntless Philip de Bresse recognised
that he must completely alter his tactics
should he wish to return to his native
land ; that his only chance of obtaining a
voice in his country's government lay in
submission to the Regent and absolute
deference to her decrees. Blanche was
anxious to gain over to her side this restless

but powerful member of her husband's family, and with much tact and diplomacy she gained her point.   Philip, recognising the advantage of joining his influence and arms to support the cause of Savoy against that of Saluces, determined to act as a faithful relative and subject of the House of Savoy.   He gave up his hostile attitude, received as a reward the post of Governor-General of Piedmont, and fulfilled his duties nobly and faithfully.

That danger overcome, Blanche hastened to remove the next great peril threatening the state, on the side of Saluces. Advised by her cousin Lodovico the Moor, and convinced by her own clear judgment that no other course was possible, she ordered her troops to evacuate the lands of Saluces.   She signed a treaty by which those same lands were restored to the Marquis ; the vexed question of the homage due from the Marquis to the Duke was waived by the Duchess ; and though some writers have described the whole transaction as an act of treachery and self - interest on the part of Lodovico

Sforza, the fact that it proved of lasting benefit to Savoy may somewhat exonerate the " Moor."

Another anxiety for Blanche at the moment of assuming the Regency was the state of the exchequer.   Its empty condition has already been alluded to.   A proof of the utter lack of either money or credit stands revealed in the fact that on the death of Duke Charles I. the mourning for the Duchess and her Court had to be paid for with borrowed money.   Blanche's high sense of honour and justice sought at once for a remedy to so crippling and mortifying a state of things.   She resolved without delay to reduce the number of her household, and to cut down all the expenses relating to her immediate service.

Among the pages who at this crisis left the ducal Court was one whose name yet thrills the hearts of all who hear it, and awakens in every breast a feeling of chivalry and romance.   And yet under the name of " Pierre du Terrail " few perhaps will recognise the " Seigneur de Bayard," the *Chevalier sans peur et sans reproche* ["the knight without fear and without reproach"]. The young knight, or rather page (for it was in that capacity he had served at the Court at Turin), had been presented to Charles I., at Chambéry in the spring of 1486. His name, spelt and misspelt as "Bainard," "Bairard," "de Beard," "Baicard," and his nickname, too, of "Piquet," occur again and again in the Court accounts, even after the Duke's death, when he appears in the list of those who put on mourning for his dead master. It was not till the beginning of October, 1490, that Bayard left the service of Savoy. That he left with marks of affection and respect is evident from the following entry, which shows how the departing page was provided with all that he could require for his journey and his apparel when Duchess Blanche could no longer retain him near her person : "Item. the 28th day of the said month of September of the above year [1490] was delivered to Master William Sorge, tailor of the said my lord, a yard and a quarter of black satin for making a jacket for

Piquet the page, who goeth to his uncle
Monseigneur of Grenoble ; and Madame
has given him notice and has commanded
that he shall be dressed." Besides other
articles of wearing apparel which are entered in the account, he was also presented
with a gelding valued at twenty florins, and
ten florins were given him in money. To
complete his equipment another entry on
the 8th of October states that "a pair of
laced buskins of cowhide," were ordered,
"with double soles for Piquet the page
when he went to France," and that they
cost three florins. Bayard was once again
to visit the Court of Duchess Blanche, but
that was not till he was in the service of
the King of France, and had wielded
against Italy the sword which he had
learned to handle at the Court of Turin.

It is curious to note how one and all of
the courtiers (and I use the word in the sense
of those who held some post at the Court)
were provided with clothes at the Duchess's
expense. While satins, silks, and velvets
were purchased at Venice, Genoa, and
in France, the linen was bought in Hol-

land. The cloth all came from France, from whence—who can deny that every kind of history repeats itself?—the fashions were also obtained; and the Court tailor, Pierre Roche, who evidently still retained his place and patronage, went now and again to Paris to learn the latest and most graceful modes, and brought back for the Duchess's special edification, not merely patterns and figures, but tiny dolls, completely and elaborately dressed, so that his royal mistress should make no mistake as to the fashion and cut in which her own garments were to be modelled! For, in spite of state cares and occupations, once the first years of mourning were ended, the Duchess was not indifferent as to the splendour and brilliancy of her Court; feasts, banquets, and theatricals, were all held in turn, and the visit of a relative or an ambassador from some foreign and friendly court became at once an occasion for merriment and rejoicing, as did also the wedding of any of Blanche's maids of honour or other personal attendants. But though she in-

dulged in all the gaiety and revelling
possible at Court for the sake of her people and to keep up the traditions of the
House of Savoy, she doubtless found a
greater pleasure and solace in the religious
services which she attended so frequently,
and in the many acts of charity and devo-

SEAL OF THOMAS I., COUNT OF SAVOY.

tion to which, notwithstanding her innumerable other duties, she always dedicated
much of her time and attention. In Lent,
and especially in Holy Week, she set a
good example by attending with great
pomp all the prescribed services. Large
and numerous were the alms which she dis-

tributed to the poor, who thronged around her on those occasions, certain that they would not go away unrelieved from her gracious presence.   Her motherly heart also sought comfort in constantly offering up images of wax of the weight of her children. She hoped to gain by these votive emblems some improvement in the health of her son and daughter, both of whom were extremely delicate.   It was the little Duke respecting whose condition the gravest fears were entertained.   The Duchess, however, far from coddling the boy or indulging in over-precautions and pamperings, tried every means to harden and invigorate his feeble frame.   Before he was five years old she had him taught to ride, and " Il Duchino " was soon pronounced an accomplished horseman by all who saw him careering about on his pony, perfectly at home in the saddle.

But apart from her preoccupation as to her children's health there was a cloud on the political horizon which haunted Blanche and filled her with doubts and misgivings as to the course of action she would now have to adopt.   The intention of Charles VIII. of France to descend upon Italy and to possess himself of Naples, as the first step towards further conquests, had so far taken shape that this monarch was about to start on that ill-fated expedition, fraught with evil to everyone who took any part in it.   Charles's ambassadors had been travelling throughout Italy, inquiring at the different courts as to those who would receive the King and help him forward on his way.   The answers had, on the whole, been favourable, no one venturing to oppose single-handed His Most Christian Majesty.   No concord—worthy of the name—existed at that moment in Italy to unite against the common foe. Where all were opening their doors and highways, the Duchess of Savoy could not be the only one to shut hers.   And, besides, the advice—hardly removed from an order—that she received from Lodovico the Moor, her chief councillor and ally, left her no choice but to welcome the French King and assume a pleasure, if she felt it not, at the prospect of his arrival.

The accusation brought forward, against Blanche, of not having closed the passes of Savoy to Charles VIII. and his army, is a most unjust one. To have done so would have been to lay herself open to the enmity of Milan, Montferrat, Saluces, and her colleague and uncle, Philip de Bresse. Charles would have made for himself a passage through other and more friendly states. The only Italian ruler that might have seconded her opposition would have been Alfonso of Naples, and he was too distant an ally to have been of real help. Blanche had but one course open to her. This course was to welcome Charles with what appearance of cordiality she could; to arrange that his passage through her states should bring as little harm as possible to her subjects; and to speed him on his way with all the hurry consistent with diplomacy and courtesy.

On Friday, September 5, 1494, Charles VIII. made his solemn entry into Turin, when a company of lunatics went out to meet him, not, as might have been supposed, to induce him by the irony of such

a reception to desist from his mad undertaking, but because " it was a most ancient
custom in the city on all solemn occasions,
and one employed when Charlemagne,
raised to the Imperial rank by Pope Leo
III., came by our Alps to Turin."[1]   The
Duchess, accompanied by her son, rode out
by the "Porta di Susa" to receive her
guest, followed by the clergy, the Council of Piedmont, the members of the Uni-
versity, the heads of the Communes, and a
large crowd of nobles, burghers, and work-
men.   The little Duke, on horseback, had
on his head a helmet; the Duchess was
mounted on a steed led by six squires, all
dressed in gold brocade.   Blanche had on
a robe of antique cloth of gold[2] studded
with big sapphires, diamonds, rubies, and
other precious stones; her hair, *coiffé* in
a high erection over her head (as was the
fashion at that time), glistened with gems
and gold ; on her neck and arms were rows
upon rows of Oriental pearls.   Surely a
dangerous display of jewels and riches to

---

[1] Ferrero di Lavriano, *Storia di Torino*, ii., 494.
[2] See Appendix.

make before a needy man and a monarch whose cry was always for money and whose delicacy was never offended in whatever form it was offered him! Around the Duchess came a host of maids of honour, dressed so gorgeously that "nothing more sumptuous could have been conceived"; behind them again came a crowd of knights, barons, lords, squires, and pages.   With this brave escort the King entered Turin, where the streets were hung with cloth of gold, tapestry, and silk.   Here and there the procession halted to witness some miracle play, together with representations of historic and legendary scenes; bands of music struck up their strains of welcome. Thus the royal party arrived at last at the castle.   Here the Duchess, her young son, and Philip de Bresse tendered their homage to King Charles, the little Duke bade him welcome in a set speech, and so courteous and affectionate was the greeting given and the offers of help and service tendered that Charles is said to have shed tears of delight and emotion.

The following morning a long interview

Carolus Joannes Amedeus Sabaudiæ Dux VI. Cypri Rex, a Beroldo XXIV. Caroli I. filius. Taurini natus die 24. Iunij. Anno 1489. nouem mensium infantulus à Patre relinquitur sub tutelâ Blanchæ Ferratensis. Carolo VIII. Francorum Regi, superatis Alpibus, ac Neapolitanæ oppidis, Italiam ingredienti obuiam fuit, elegantiquæ oratione se, & generoso equo insidens aurum ad expeditionem Italicam Regis placitis adeò comitem sese obtulit, ut Rex ipse præ gaudio illachrymasse uisus sit. Septimo ætatis anno immaturam mortem oppetijt die 16. Aprilis, anno 1496.

I. C. Diæus Amedensis del.   I. Manuer sculps Taurini 17

took place between the King, Blanche, and the little Duke, when, according to Brantôme, the King, whose devotion to the fair sex is well known, "monstroit en apparence estre au cour blessé" by the grace and beauty of the Duchess. Though his gallant overtures met with no response on her side, she yet so far acceded to his piteous entreaties for money as to hand over to him all her jewels, in the belief that this pledge of her good-will would hasten his departure and that her jewels would eventually be restored to her. No mention occurs as to any restitution of this noble loan of the Duchess. Still her relief must have been great when that same day, after dinner, the French King took leave of his loving cousins of Savoy and set off for Chieri, on his way to conquer the Kingdom of Naples.

This is not the place to speak of the expedition of Charles VIII. into Italy, of his conquest of Naples, of the League at last formed against him by Italian states and princes to drive him out of the Peninsula, nor of the climax brought about by

the battle of Fornovo (July 6, 1495).
But an incident during that battle relates
to the House of Savoy, and therefore
must not be omitted. When Charles VIII.
left Turin, besides carrying off Duchess
Blanche's jewel-case, he also took with him
another rich possession in the shape of a
horse, presented to him by the young
Duke, and that was called " Savoie."
This horse is spoken of by all the writers
of the time, and Philip de Commines thus
describes a colloquy he had with the King
only a few minutes before the battle of
Fornovo : " Je vins a luy le trovay armé
de toutes pieces et monté sur le plus beau
cheval que j'aye veu de mon temps appele
Savoye ; plusieurs disoyent qu'il estoit
cheval de Bresse ; le duc Charles de Savoye le luy avoit donné : et estoit noir et
n'avoit qu'un æil et estoit moyen cheval
de bonne grandeur pour celui qui estoit
monté dessus." [1] To the swiftness of this
horse Charles VIII. owed his safety at the
battle of Fornovo, and though history
may lament that " Savoye " was possessed

[1] *Memories*, lib. viii., cap. 10.

of such fleetness of foot, his Majesty of France had cause to bless his godson for such a gift and to ascribe to him indirectly the safety of his valuable life !

The hope entertained in Italy that Charles would soon leave the country and return to his own land was not quickly fulfilled. For a month and a half Charles loitered in Piedmont, dividing his time between Turin and Chieri, and rendering Blanche's position towards her Italian neighbours an extremely difficult one. She was looked upon with suspicion as harbouring a national enemy, and though her action received the support and approbation of Lodovico the Moor, her other allies maintained an attitude of distrust towards her which was not removed till September, 1495, when Charles freed her and Italy from his undesirable presence.

His absence enabled the Duchess to devote herself at once to looking after her son's health. The whole Court repaired in October to Moncalieri, where the winter was passed sadly enough, no change for the better making itself perceptible in

the young Duke's condition.   The remedies employed for the little patient were
certainly some of the strangest that could
be imagined, and consisted of rose-water,
"eau de Mélisse," extract of violets, costly
wines, while with these different liquids
were mixed powdered gold, fragments of
jacinths, of rubies, garnets, pearls, white
and pink coral, sandalwood, camphor,
amber, musk, aniseed, cinnamon, and burnt
horn.   All these compounds were jumbled
up in such a medley that the wonder is
not so much that the child did not recover
as that he ever lived to take a second and
third dose of these odd concoctions.   Other
remedies of baths, extracts of meat and
game, ointments, and the like were also
tried, but all was in vain, and on the
16th of April, 1496, notwithstanding the
prayers, votive offerings, and assiduous
care of his mother, Charles John Amadeus
died.   The little corpse was embalmed,
and buried with much state in the Church
of St. Mary at Moncalieri, while his subjects wept not so much for the loss of a
Prince who was too young to have im-

pressed them either for good or for bad,
as from the fact that his death removed
from them the wise and beneficent rule
of his mother, Blanche of Montferrat.

The cup of sorrow of which the poor
Duchess Blanche had drunk so deeply was
not yet entirely drained. Her daughter,
Yolande Lodovica, was still left to her,
and to this child her thoughts and attention were now altogether devoted. Blanche
had given up the Regency immediately on
her son's death, and had done all in her
power to insure the peaceful accession of
Philip de Bresse, her children's great-uncle,
and the only surviving son of Duke Lodovico and Anna of Cyprus. Her life
then was passed quietly at Turin, a town
for which she always felt and manifested
a strong affection, and which owed to her
its final recognition as the definite capital
of the House of Savoy. Here she took
part in the betrothal of her daughter Yolande to Philibert, Prince of Piedmont,
and eldest son of the reigning Duke
Philip. The relationship and the youth
of the young couple made their actual

union an impossibility for the time being, and though both these obstacles were such as time and papal dispensations could easily have removed, some historians have denied the fact of this marriage. That their relation was considered as such by the members of the ducal family there can be no doubt. The medal here given is a proof that it ranked as a marriage when the token was struck to commemorate the union of the two families of the House of Savoy.

MEDAL OF PHILIBERT II. AND YOLANDE LODOVICA.

Three years after this betrothal, to satisfy the entreaties of Philibert, who had set up his Court at Geneva, Blanche went in great state with Yolande to visit the young Prince. The visit lasted several months : but during the whole time Blanche's anxieties knew no bounds, for the affianced bride languished and drooped day by day. On September 12, 1499, the child died at Geneva, aged little more than twelve years.

Duchess Blanche had now indeed reached the culminating point of her sorrows. She had not yet attained to the age of thirty, yet death had robbed her of all those she loved best, leaving her a childless widow with a future of sadness and solitude before her, all the harder to bear after the life of activity and stir to which she had been accustomed. Now all was taken from her, and the brave spirit, that had worked with such energy and interest for her people's good and for her children's welfare, had to face the dreariness of a lonely life with no given occupations or duties beyond those she might choose to form for herself. No wonder that even Blanche's courage failed for a moment before the depressing outlook. Her health began to suffer, so she determined to leave Geneva, where the associations of all she had gone through were more than she could bear. She removed by slow stages to Turin, thinking that she would make her home there, but that, too, was so haunted by memories of the past that she could not bear it. She accordingly retired to Carignan, where, far from the turmoils of public life and its cares, she could find the seclusion and quiet which were now all she craved. Here, occupied in looking after the property adjoining the castle, and busy with her household and domestic duties, she lived in tranquillity and retirement. The calm monotony of her life was now occasionally interrupted by the visit of some illustrious person who had known her in her brighter and more prosperous days, and who still wished to offer her the respect and admiration which she never failed to inspire in all who knew her. King Louis XII. of France came twice to visit her; Francis I. did likewise; and the peerless Bayard, who for four years had served as page to her husband, and

VIEW OF CARIGNAN.

whose instincts of chivalry and knighthood had been fostered and developed at
the Court of Savoy, came also to offer his
homage to the widow of his old master.

This visit took place early in 1500.   It
may be that it was prompted as much by
the knight's desire to see once more the
lady who was his "dear and only love" as
to pay his respects to the Duchess Blanche.
This lady, who had been one of Blanche's
maids of honour when Bayard was a page,
was now the Countess of Frossasco, wife
of Bertolino di Montbel, majordomo of
the palace.   In their early youth the page
and the maid of honour had plighted their
troth to each other; but the page had
gone off to France, and the maiden, oblivious of her youthful engagement, had
married a worthy and respectable gentleman of Savoy.   Now, however, when they
met again, the old love—but tempered with
chaste and noble sentiments—revived once
more.   The lady called upon the knight,
whose fame was now of world-wide renown, to give some proof of his skill and
valour and in this way to do honour to

the Court of Savoy where he had been
brought up. The knight thereupon replied : " You know how I have always
loved and honoured you ; tell me what I
must do to please my lady the Duchess,
you before all, and also this goodly company."   The Countess suggested that he
should hold a tourney, to which Bayard
agreed, saying : " You are the lady who
first possessed my heart ; I know I can
never hope for more than to kiss your
mouth and your hand ; that I should ask
more from you would be useless ; and, on
my soul, I would rather die than urge you
to dishonour.   Give me, I pray you, one
of your wristbands, for that is necessary
to me."   The lady gave the desired pledge,
the tourney was proclaimed, and Bayard
offered the wristband, to which was fastened a ruby of the value of one hundred
ducats, as a prize to the knight who should
excel in three tilts with the lance and in
twelve sword-strokes.   It is needless to
add that Bayard excelled all the other
knights, and to him, consequently, the
prize was awarded.

But he, blushing deeply, declared that if he had won the prize, the merit lay not with him but with her who had prepared the reward. So he prayed her, therefore, to deliver it to him whom she deemed most worthy of such an honour. On this, the Countess, after expressing her thanks to Bayard, said to him: " Since you affirm that it is owing to my wristband that you have come out victorious in the lists, I will preserve it all my life for love of you ; but if you will not have the ruby, then let it be given to the Lord of Mondragon whom all declare to have been, after you, the bravest knight." This having been done, a great ball took place, and rejoicings and feasts went on for the next five or six days. After this entertainment, Bayard and the French knights took leave of Blanche, marvelling at their wonderful reception. They asserted that never had they met a prince or a princess who had shown such courtesy and hospitality to her guests as this Duchess had done.

After this, Blanche's life followed the even tenor of its way for seven years.

But occasional festivals brightened the tranquil stateliness of her Court life, as for instance in 1504, when a brilliant entertainment for the wedding of one of Blanche's maids of honour with one of Duke Philibert's chief gentlemen was celebrated at Carignan, at which the Duke, his wife, Margaret of Austria, and several members of the ducal family were present.   But these gaieties were of rare occurrence.   The Duchess was for the most part left undisturbed to the cultivation of silk-worms and the improvement of the silk trade, which interested her greatly, and owes much of its development and success to her.   The cultivation of silk-worms (now such a source of income to most Italian landowners) was then only beginning to make its way.   Duchess Blanche gave a decided impetus to the growing commerce.   While she was still Regent she had set up a silk factory in Turin, and had also sent for a woman from Greece to teach the art of weaving, for a dyer from Barcelona, and for the best dyes and colours from Venice.

The Duchess did not disdain the homely duties of housekeeping, but personally superintended the making of syrups, jams, and other preserves with the keenest zest, and afterwards enjoyed sending these specimens of her handicraft to her friends and relatives.   To the Duke of Savoy she sent presents of dried prunes and almonds, of quince jam and another preserved fruit called "zesti," which seems to have been a specialty of Carignan.   She also devoted much of her time to her domestic pets, for whom she had always a marked affection, and was much occupied with the rearing of several breeds of dogs, on which she set great store, and which were declared to be of great value.   Several of her letters are still extant which prove how diligently she busied herself over all the affairs entrusted to her control ; they allude to the injunctions she gave to her different agents, inciting them to greater activity or reproving them when they neglected their duties.

Thus the years slipped quietly and quickly away ; but Blanche, notwithstanding the gallant way she had faced her trials and carved out for herself a life full of healthy pursuits and of wide-spreading good, had suffered too deeply to live to "a good old age." She was now only about forty-seven years old, but the trials and sorrows which had so heavily overshadowed her early youth had sapped the spring of her life. Her health began to fail early in 1518, and Blanche, feeling that her days were numbered, determined to put her affairs in order. In February, 1519, she drew up her will. She bequeathed all her possessions absolutely to Charles III., Duke of Savoy; soon after this, on the 31st of March of this same year, she died. Her funeral took place at Carignan, when her body, dressed in dark-coloured velvet studded with gold, was buried, according to her desire, in the Church of St. Mary adjoining the Augustinian convent which had been largely endowed and enriched by her.

The testimony passed on Blanche of Montferrat by the old chronicler, Paradin, is a fitting close to this short and in-

complete sketch of the Savoyard Duchess,
and runs as follows: "This good lady
knew well that in this Duchy and House
of Savoy tyrants had never found a footing; and that a grand administration lay
entirely in piety and justice. To which
two things she gave such good heed that
in her time the good were never oppressed,
nor the evil advantaged."[1]

[1] See Appendix.

SEAL OF EDWARD, COUNT OF SAVOY.

APPENDIX

VOL. I., P. 11.—To Amadeus III. is due the foundation of the Abbey of Hautecombe, on the Lake of Bourget. Here he placed some monks from Aulps, which was originally an offshoot from the monastery of Molesme. The abbey, founded in 1125, was for a long time the sepulchre of the House of Savoy. Destroyed by ruthless hands at the time of the French Revolution, it was rebuilt by King Charles Felix and his wife, Queen Maria Christina, in a debased style.

VOL. I., P. 129.—"*Grande chronique* de Matthieu Paris. *Tradit en Français* par A. Huillard-Breholles, *accompagnée de notes et precedée d'une Introduction* par M. Le Duc de Luynes. Paris, 1840*"*; and "*The History of England, written in French*, by Mr. Rapin de Thoyras; *translated into English with additional notes* by Mr. Tindal, M.A., Vicar of Great Waltham in Essex. London, 1732." I owe the privilege of consulting the former of these works to Mr. Bain, 1 Haymarket, London, and the latter to the Rev. E. Blythe, to both of whom my thanks are due.

VOL. I., P. 139.—"An obscure meaning and an incomplete sentence," says M. de Luynes in his note, and one for which he can offer no satisfactory explanation. I would suggest that it might refer to the barons whose estates formed part of the ever-growing town of London, and whose titles were derived from those estates.

Vol. I., p. 158.—The name of this princess was simply the feminine of " Sanche."   But the play of words invented by the courtiers must doubtless have pleased a princess who hailed from the land of the " gay science," " lo gay saber."   The Earl of Cornwall, following the example of his uncle, Richard Cœur de Lion, busied himself in composing in the Provençal tongue, and esteemed it an honour to be reckoned among the troubadours.

Vol. I., p. 177.— The material relating to Boniface is taken almost entirely from M. Paris's chronicle, with frequent quotations translated from the French publication to which such constant reference has already been made.

Vol. I., p. 190.—" Eya, per Christum, predecessores mei aulam istam cum magnis expensis fecerunt, sed expensas ad illam construendam nisi de summa mutuata non invenerunt.   Videtur quidem mihi, quod ego illam feci : quia illorum debita persolvi."—Wharton, *Anglia Sacra*, i., p. 11.

Vol. I., p. 191.—A bull of Pope Gregory XVI., dated September 1, 1838, enrolls Boniface, Archbishop of Canterbury, and Count Humbert III. among the Beatified, and a long account of the lives of these two princes is given in the *Vita de beati Humberta e Bonifacio di Savoia* (Torino : Stamferia Reale, 1839). These acts of beatification were granted by Pope Gregory XVI. at the request of King Charles Albert.

VOL. I., P. 192.—The greater part of this chapter is taken from "Cronicque de Savoye" in the *Monum. Stor. Patr.*, tom. i., col. 275 ; and from "Datta Spedizione" in *Oriente di Amadeo VI., Conte di Savoia, Provata con Documenti Inediti.* Torino, 1826.

VOL. I., P. 227.—"In the collection of coins belonging to His Majesty the King of Sardinia is a golden doubloon, struck under the reign of Victor Amadeus I. [1630–37], on one side of which appears his effigy and on the other four love-knots, placed in the form of a cross, in the centre of which is the shield of Savoy. They are alternate with four groups of hands interlaced and surrounded by this motto : *Fædere et religione tenemur.*"— Frederick D. Hartland, *The Times*, London, Dec. 7, 1855.

VOL. I., P. 228.—The Conte Verde in his will founded and endowed the Chartreuse of Pierre Chastel, where fifteen monks (the number being chosen in honour of the fifteen joyous mysteries of the Blessed Virgin) were to live and to pray for the souls of the Knights of the Collar.

VOL. I., P. 256.—On the death of Amadeus VII., not only were accusations made against Granville, the physician, Pierre de Lompnes the Chemist, and the Countess Bonne la Grande, but one of the leading courtiers, Othon de Grandson, was also made responsible for being concerned in suggesting the murder. This speedily assumed a most serious aspect. Amadeus VIII. was induced to have Grandson subjected to a judicial inquiry. No suspicion of guilt, however, could be attached to him. Six years after the death of the Red Count, he was charged a second time with this offence by Gerard d'Estavayer. An appeal was made to a wager of battle, the judicial combat of *un jugement de Dieu*. A sanguinary encounter took place August 7, 1397, at Bresse, in which Grandson was killed by d'Estavayer. Upon this, the Grandson estates were escheated to the state under a decree of the House of Savoy.

Vol. II., p. 163.—Olivier de la Marche, *Mémoires sur la maison de Bourgogne*, ch. viii., p. 579.

Vol. II., p. 168.—Quotations from Olivier de la Marche and from Commines are also taken from a volume entitled *Choix de Chroniques et Mémoires sur l'histoire de France, avec notes biographiques*, par J. A. C. Buchon (Paris, 1830).

Vol. II., pp. 169, 171.—Ménabrea, L. *Chroniques de Yolande de France. . . . Documents inédits recueilis et mis en ordre par L. M.* Paris, 1859, Chamerot (Chambéry Imp., Putrod Fils).

Vol. II., p. 231. — Another account says that this is not probable, the Duchess having decreed that her mourning should be observed in spite of the festivities; and that, though she ordered gorgeous and coloured dresses for the little Duke and his suite, she gave instructions that her own rooms should be hung with black velvet, her dress was to be black, while all her personal attendants, ladies, squires, pages, even to the caparisons of their horses, should be dressed in either violet or black.

VOL. II., P. 247.—" La bonne dame evoit bien sceu qu'en ce duche et maison de Savoye les tyrans n'avoient jamais eu lieu ; et que les grandes administrations consistoient en piete totalement et en justice. Ausquelles deux choses elle avoit si diligemment pourvu que de son temps les bons ne furent onques oppressez ; ny les mauvais avantagez." — Paradin, Maistre Guillaume. *Cronique de Savoye.* Lyon, 1552.

INDEX

Mob plunders treasury, i., 74
Montferrat, heritage of, causes war with Spain, i., 47
Moor, Ludovico the, ii., 197
Motto of the House of Savoy, i., 226 *et seq* ; 237, ii., 251

NAME in religion, Pope-elect objects to a, ii., 49
Naples, the Bourbons expelled from, i., 91
Napoleon I.: invades Piedmont, i., 70 ; proposes a confederacy, 72
——— III.: generosity and wisdom of, i., 90 ; brings about the acquisition of Venice, 92
New Year's gifts, ii., 112, *et seq*.
Nice : acquired by House of Savoy, i., 10 ; lost for a time, 59 ; finally handed over to France, 91
Nicholas V. succeeds Eugenius IV. as Pope, i., 27, ii., 80

ODDONE : succeeds his father, Humbert I., i., 3 ; called " the husband of his wife," gaining vast possessions through his marriage, 4, 106
Oil, bath of, ii., 203
Orders instituted by Amadeus VI., i., 225

PARIS, Congress of, i., 90
Parròt, a present from Amadeus VI. to his wife, i., 220
" Passe Rose," Countess of Savoy, i., 14
Patron saint of House of Savoy, i., 102
Pembroke, Earl of, in tournament, i., 236, 240, 241
Peter I. of Savoy, i., 8, 128
——— II. of Savoy, "the little Charlemagne " : visits his niece, the Queen of England, and is given " Savoy House " by Henry III., i., 161 ; has lordships in six English counties and is made Earl of Richmond, 162 ; love of tournaments, 163 ; jealousy aroused against him, 164 ; leaves England, 165 ; tries to rescue Henry, 166; his talents, 166 ; marries Savoyards to English heiresses, 166 ; succeeds as Count (1263), 167 ; Imperial Vicar, 167 ; dressed in gold and iron, 167 ; his will, 168 ; at Chillon, 169 ; his death, 169
Philibert II. prefers Austria to France, i., 35, 36
Philip set aside from succession as Count of Savoy, i., 15
———, Count of Bresse: intrigues against his brother, Amadeus IX., i., 31, ii., 132 ; seizes Amadeus, 137 ; tricked by Yolande, 138 ; tries to rule, 139 ; wife's visit to Yolande declined, 157 ; rebels, 170 ; overcome, 170 ; troubles Blanche of Montferrat, 220 ; submits, 221 ; she appoints him Governor-General of Piedmont, 222

FRENCH HISTORY.

Old Court Life in France. By FRANCES ELLIOT. Illustrated with portraits and with views of the old châteaux. 2 vols., 8°, $4.00.   Half-calf extra, gilt tops   . $8.00

"Mrs. Elliot's is an anecdotal history of the French Court from Francis I. to Louis XIV. She has conveyed a vivid idea of the personalities touched upon, and her book contains a great deal of genuine vitality."—*Detroit Free Press.*

Woman in France During the Eighteenth Century. By JULIA KAVANAGH, author of "Madeline" etc. Illustrated with portraits on steel. 2 vols., 8°, $4.00.   Half-calf extra, gilt tops, ... $8.00

"Miss Kavanagh has studied her material so carefully, and has digested it so well, that she has been able to tell the story of Court Life in France, from the beginning of the Regency to the end of the Revolutionary period, with an understanding and a sobriety that make it practically new to English readers."—*Detroit Free Press.*

France Under Mazarin. By JAMES BRECK PERKINS. With a Sketch of the Administration of Richelieu. Portraits of Mazarin, Richelieu, Louis XIII., Anne of Austria, and Condé. 2 vols., 8° $4.00

"A brilliant and fascinating period that has been skipped, slighted, or abused by the ignorance, favoritism, or prejudice of other writers is here subjected to the closest scrutiny of an apparently judicial and candid student. . . ."—*Boston Literary World.*

A French Ambassador at the Court of Charles II.; Le Comte de Cominges. From his unpublished correspondence. Edited by J. J. JUSSERAND. With 10 illustrations, 5 being photogravures. 8°   .   . $3.50

"M. Jusserand has chosen a topic peculiarly fitted to his genius, and treated it with all the advantage to be derived, on the one hand, from his wide knowledge of English literature and English social life, and on the other, from his diplomatic experience and his freedom of access to the archives of the French Foreign Office. . . . We get a new and vivid picture of his (Cominges') life at the Court of Charles II. . . . There is not a dull page in the book."—*London Times.*

Undercurrents of the Second Empire. By ALBERT D. VANDAM, author of "An Englishman in Paris," etc. 8° $2.00

"Mr. Vandam is an Englishman, long resident in Paris, and thereby thoroughly Gallicized in his intellectual atmosphere and style of thought . . . his style is flowing and pleasing, and the work is a valuable contribution to the history of that time."—*The Churchman.*

G. P. PUTNAM'S SONS, NEW YORK AND LONDON

FRENCH HISTORY.

Jeanne D'Arc, The Maid of France. By Mrs. M. O. W. OLIPHANT. No. 17 in the Heroes of the Nations Series. Fully illustrated. Large 12° $1.50

"Mrs. Oliphant has written a charming book. The style is pleasant and simple. The reader is carried from page to page without the consciousness of fatigue. The little maid of Dom Remy has had many a biographer, but none more loving and sympathetic than our present writer."—*N. Y. Observer.*

Henry of Navarre, and the Huguenots in France. By P. F. WILLERT, M.A., Fellow of Exeter College, Oxford. No. 9 in the Heroes of the Nations Series. Fully illustrated. Large 12° $1.50

"There was room for a bright, popular history of that remarkable warrior and monarch, Henry IV. of France. This want has been well supplied by Mr. Willert, who has issued a volume of less than 500 pages, which exhibits excellent grip of the subject, and still more excellent discrimination in the dramatic representation of the central character."— *Boston Transcript.*

Louis XIV., and the Zenith of the French Monarchy. By ARTHUR HASSALL, M.A., Student of Christ Church College, Oxford. No. 14 in the Heroes of the Nations Series. Fully illustrated. Large 12°. . . $1.50

"The author of this volume has well and impartially performed his task. His style is elegant, and at the same time graphic and full of force. His book is a valuable contribution to the student of history, and it will be welcomed and valued as it deserves."—*N. Y. Christian Work.*

Napoleon, Warrior and Ruler, and the Military Supremacy of Revolutionary France. By W. O'CONNOR MORRIS. No. 8 in the Heroes of the Nations Series. Fully illustrated. Large 12° $1.50

"The book is certainly the best modern account of Napoleon in the English language."—*London Academy.*

Bertrand du Guesclin, Constable of France, His Life and Times. By ENOCH VINE STODDARD, M.D. Illustrated, 8° $1.75

"From the opening page to the last the story never flags. It is so intensely real and alive, it is so full of crash and conflict, that the reader sits like the spectator of some great historic drama."—*N. Y. Mail and Express.*

Ambroise Paré, and His Times, 1510–1590. By STEPHEN PAGET, M.A. Illustrated. 8° $2.50

Mr. Paget tells the story of the life of the great French surgeon of the sixteenth century. Ambroise Paré's life was so full of good works, adventure, and romance, that it ought to be known and honored in other countries besides France.

G. P. PUTNAM'S SONS, NEW YORK AND LONDON